I0511351

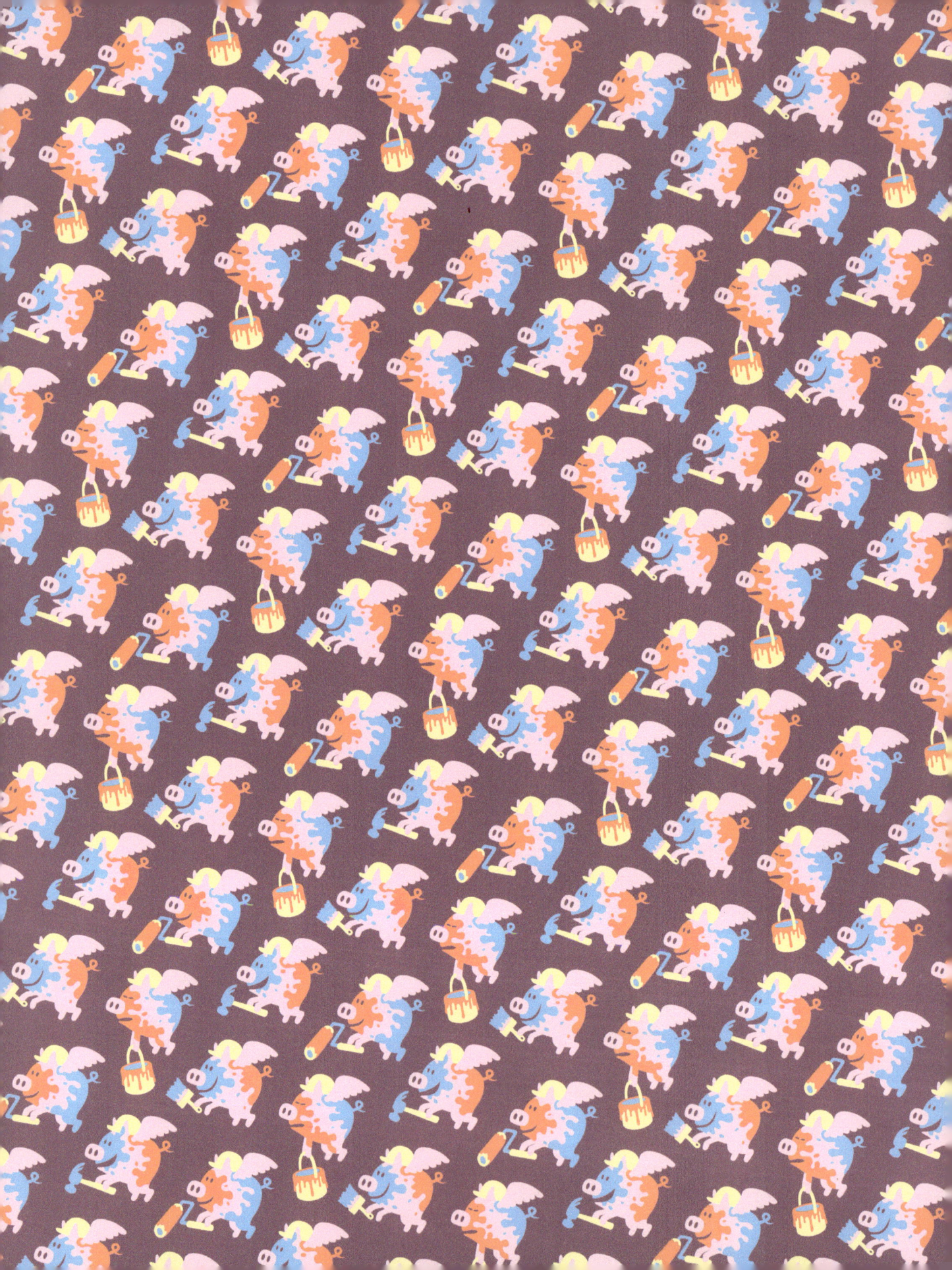

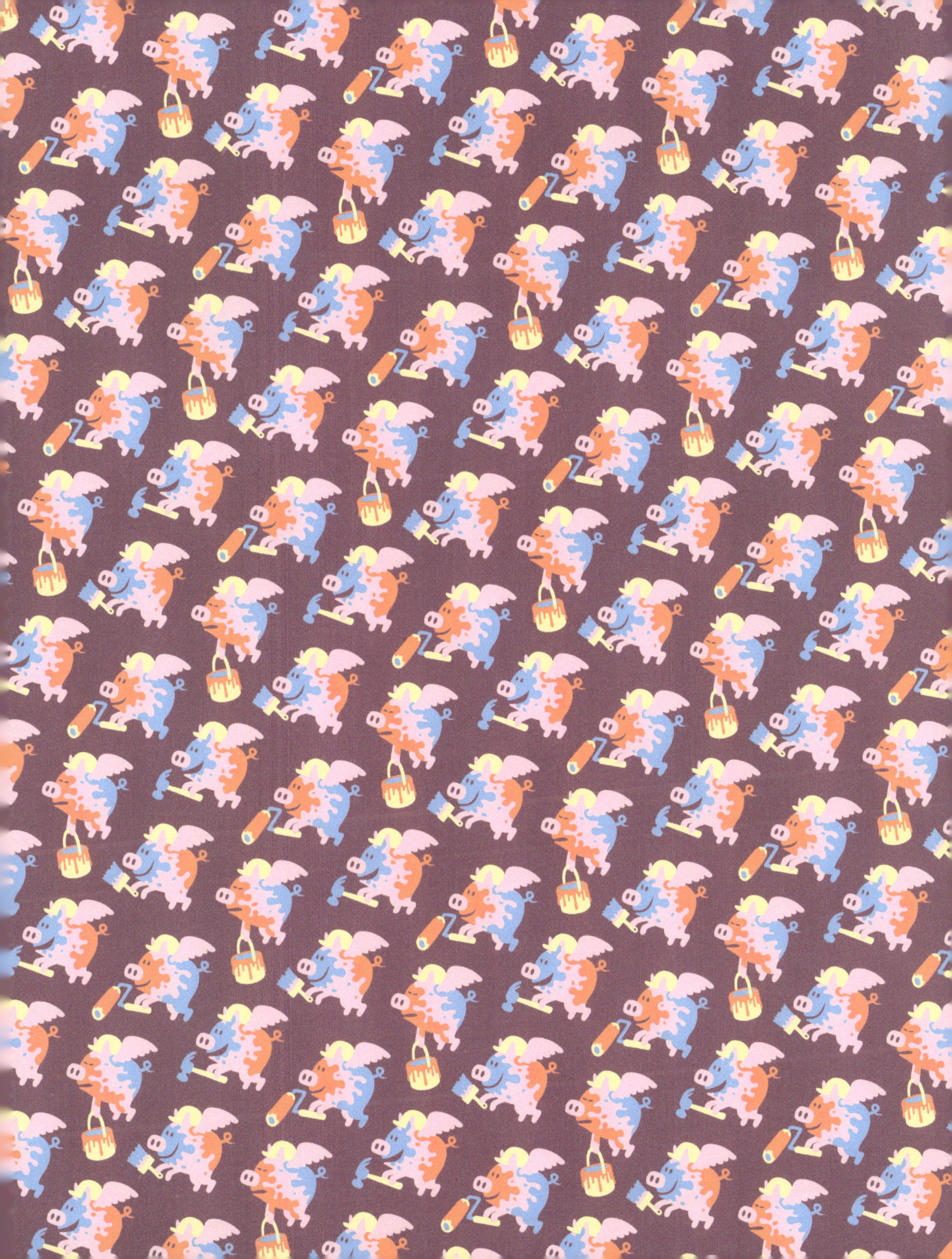

TABLE OF CONTENTS

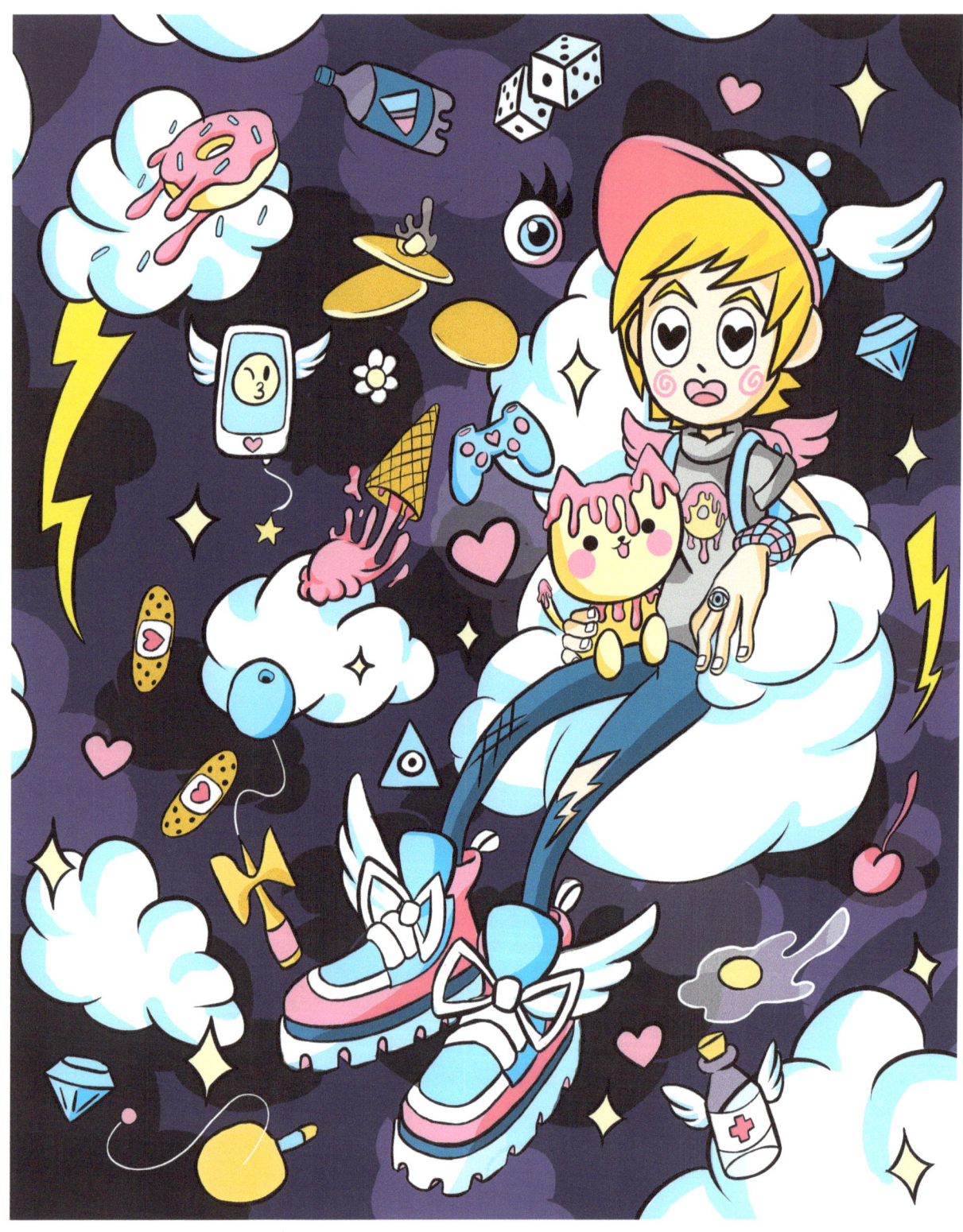

Austin Carter | streetcherub@gmail.com | streetcherub.com

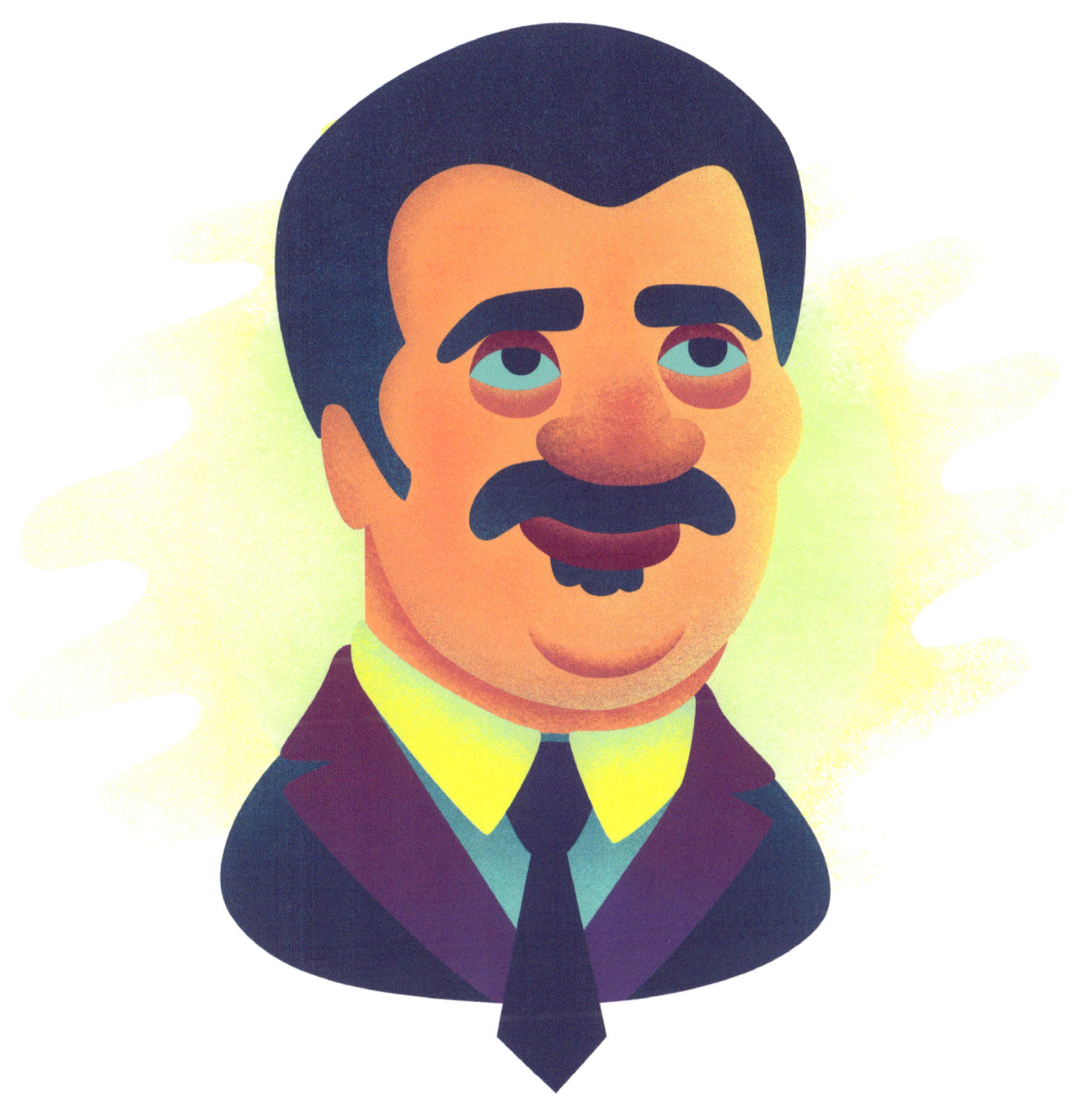

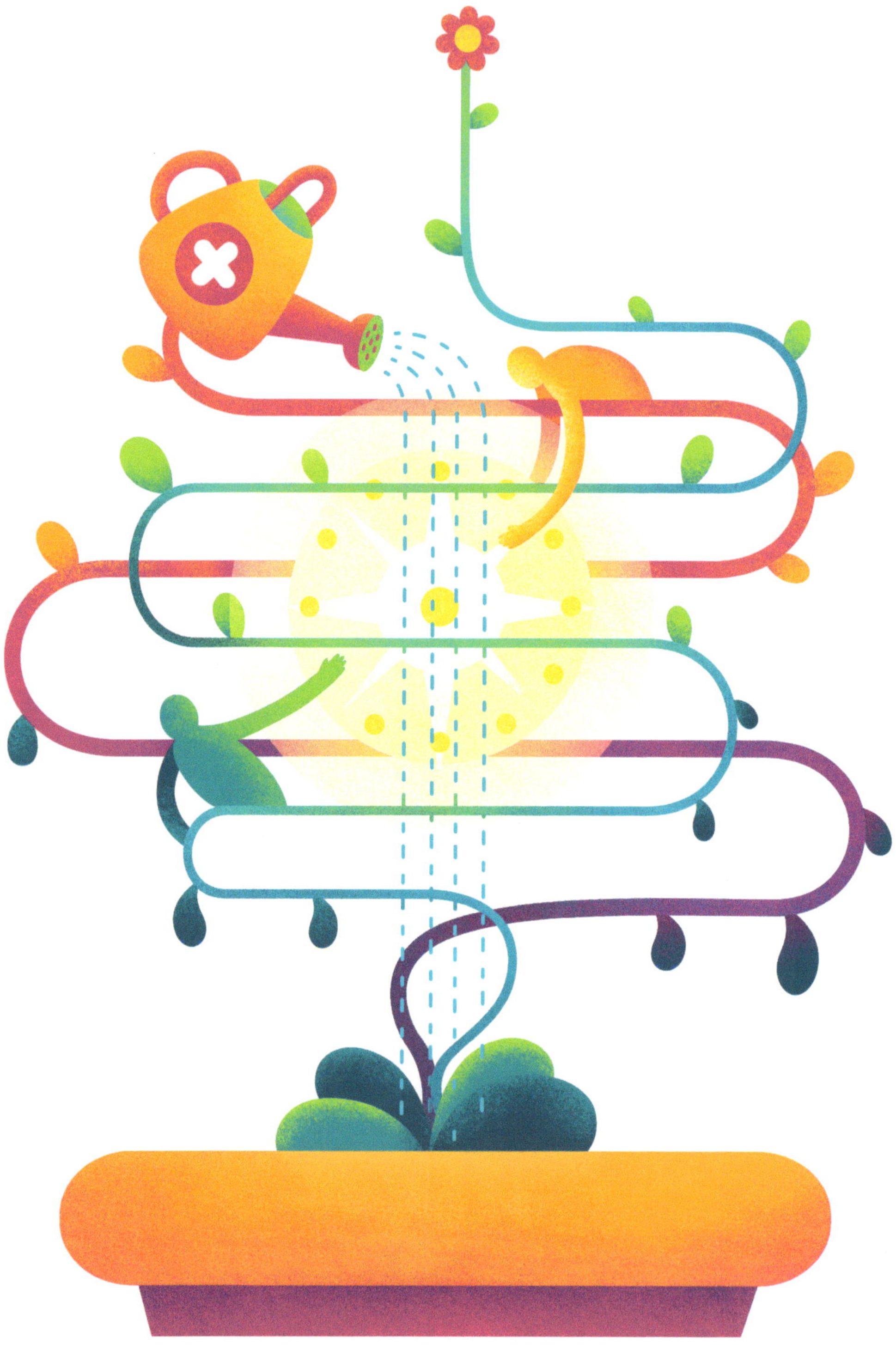

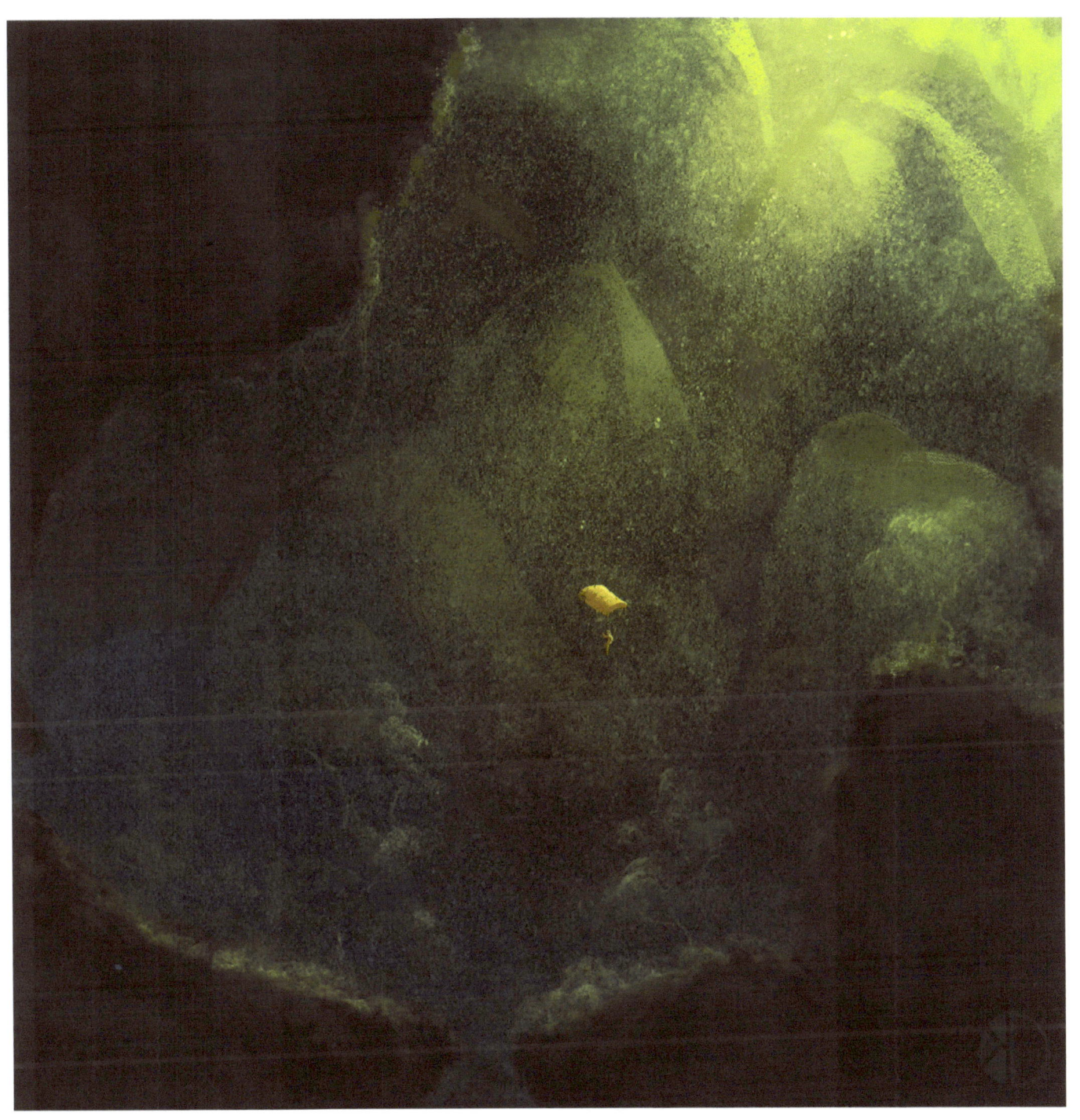

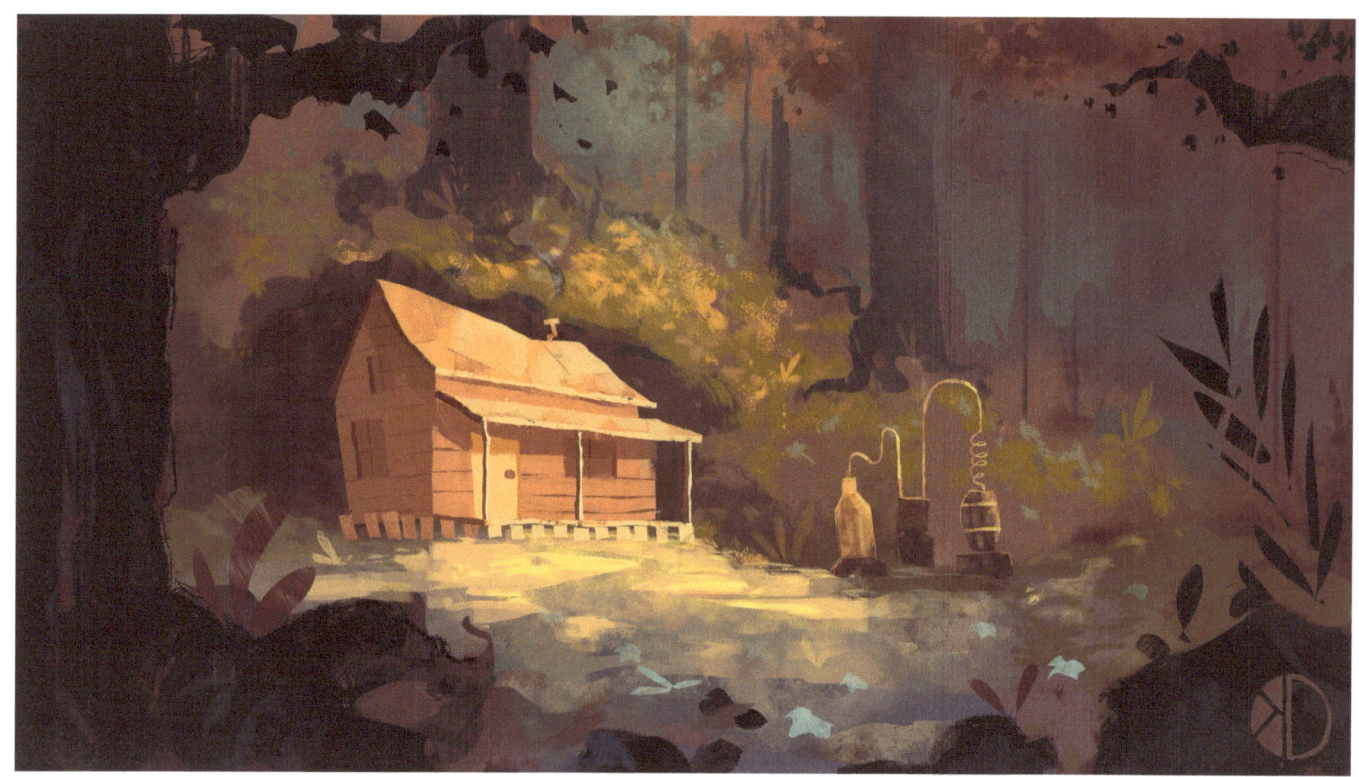

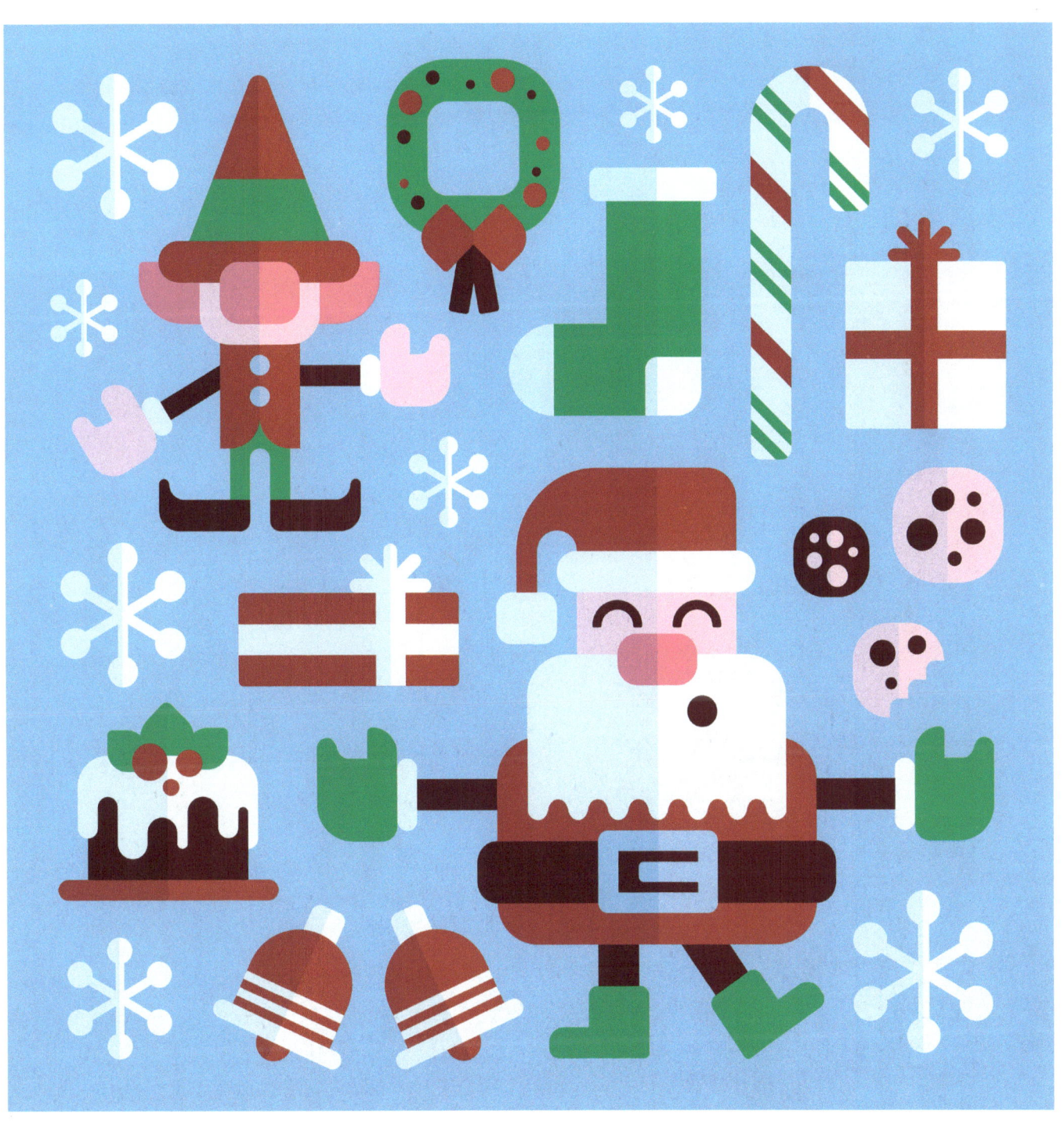

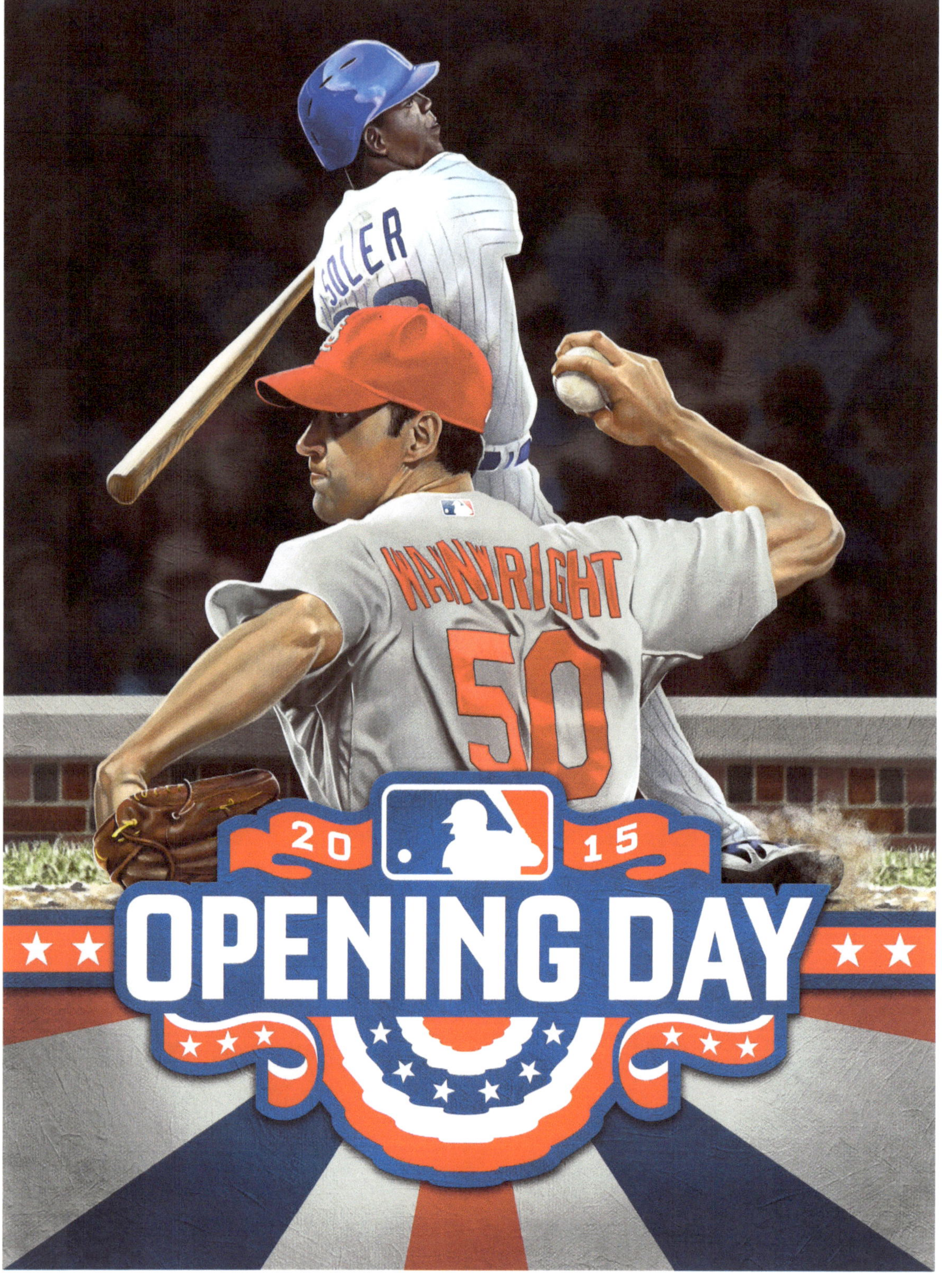

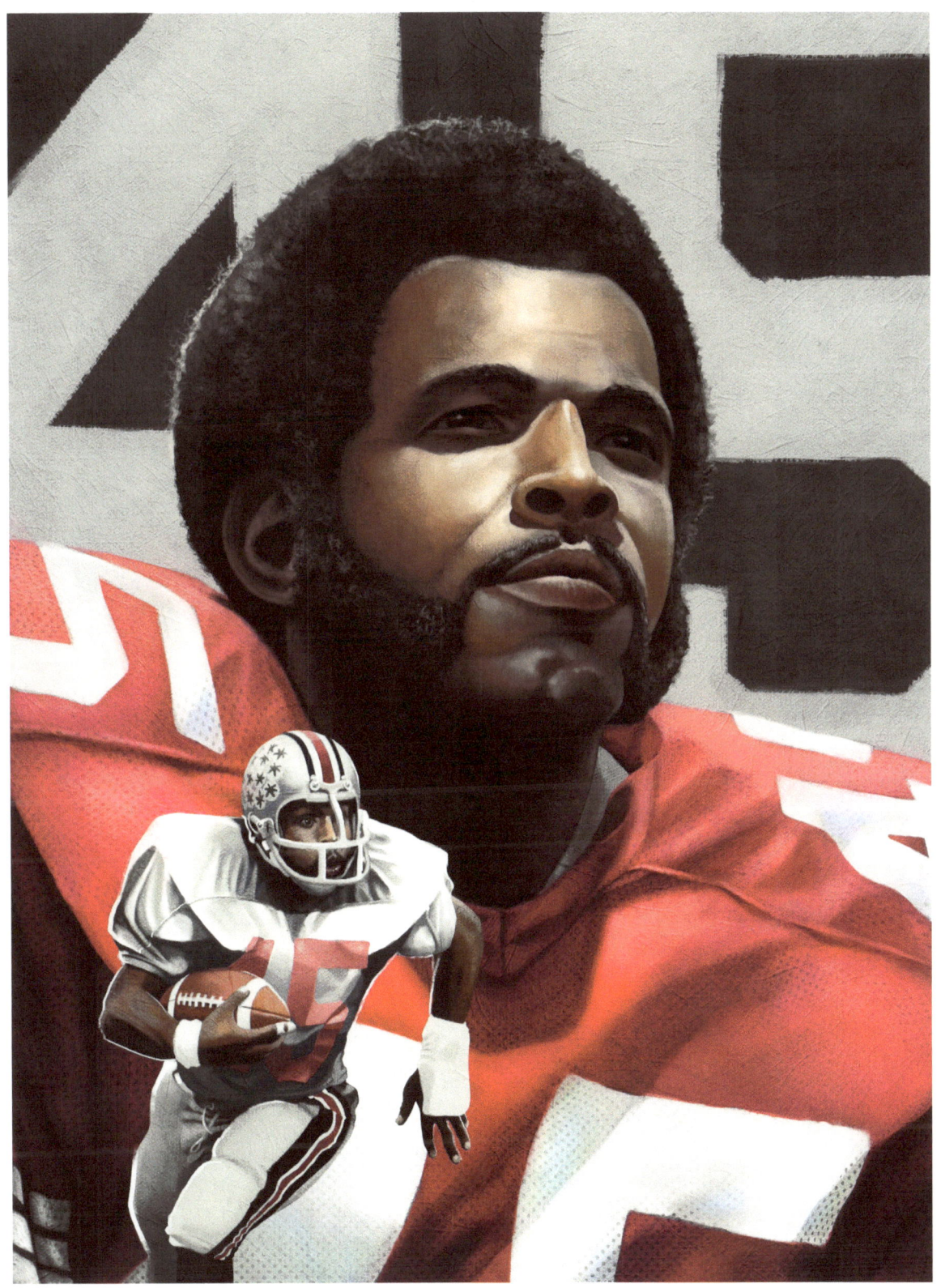

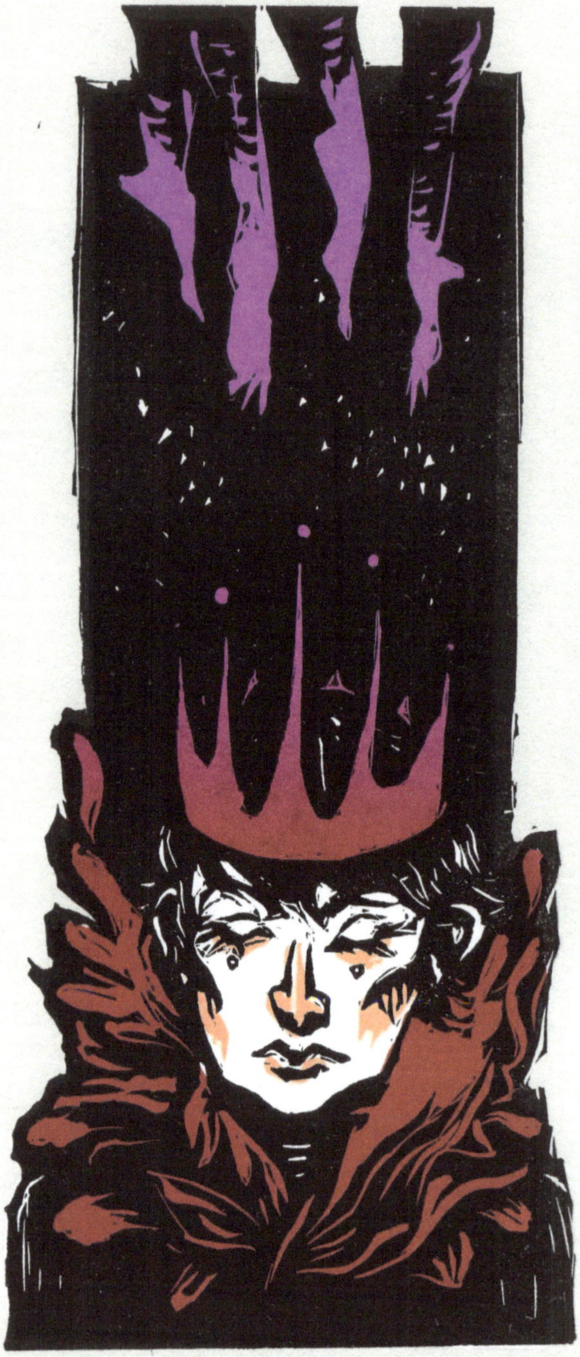

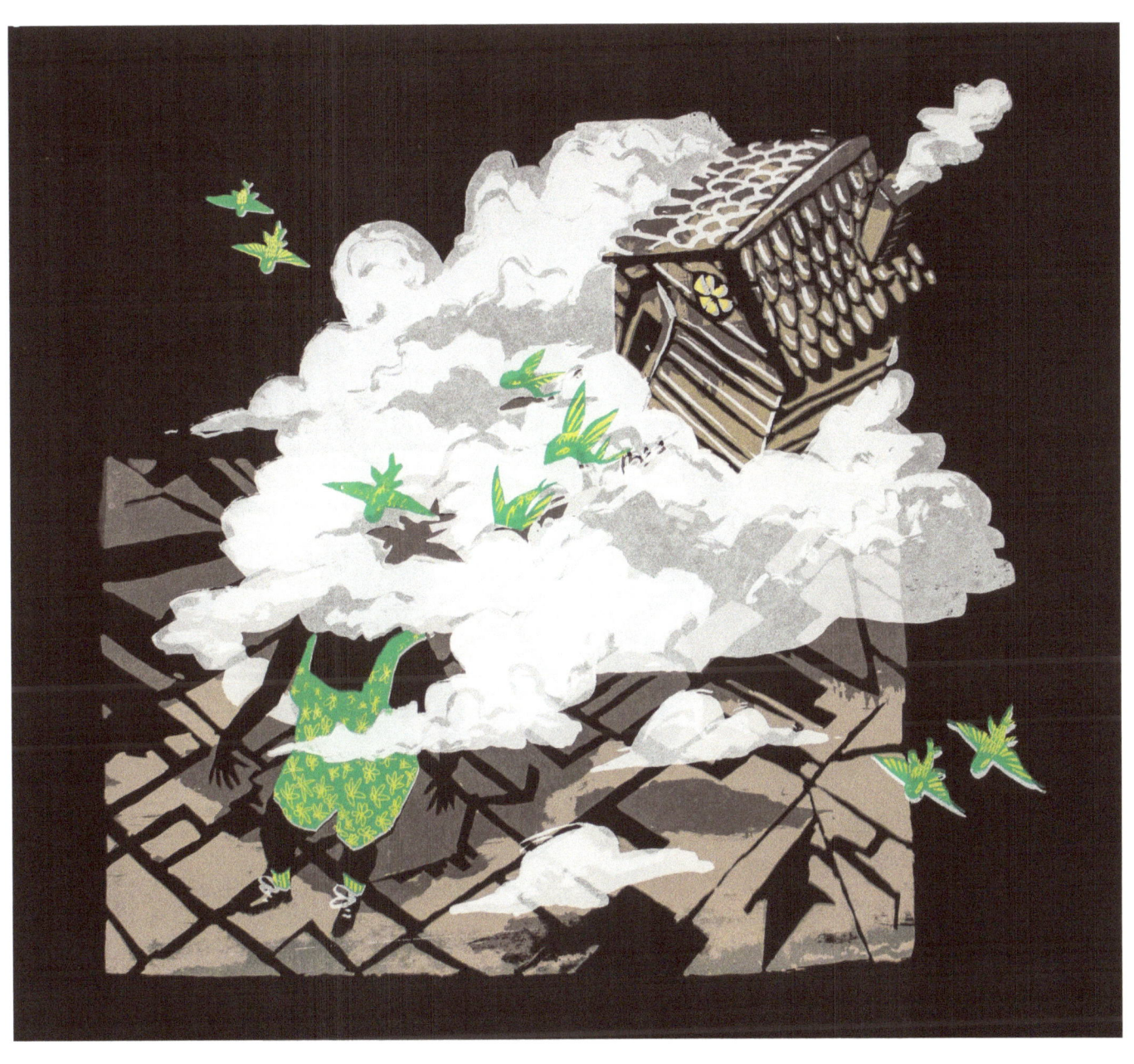

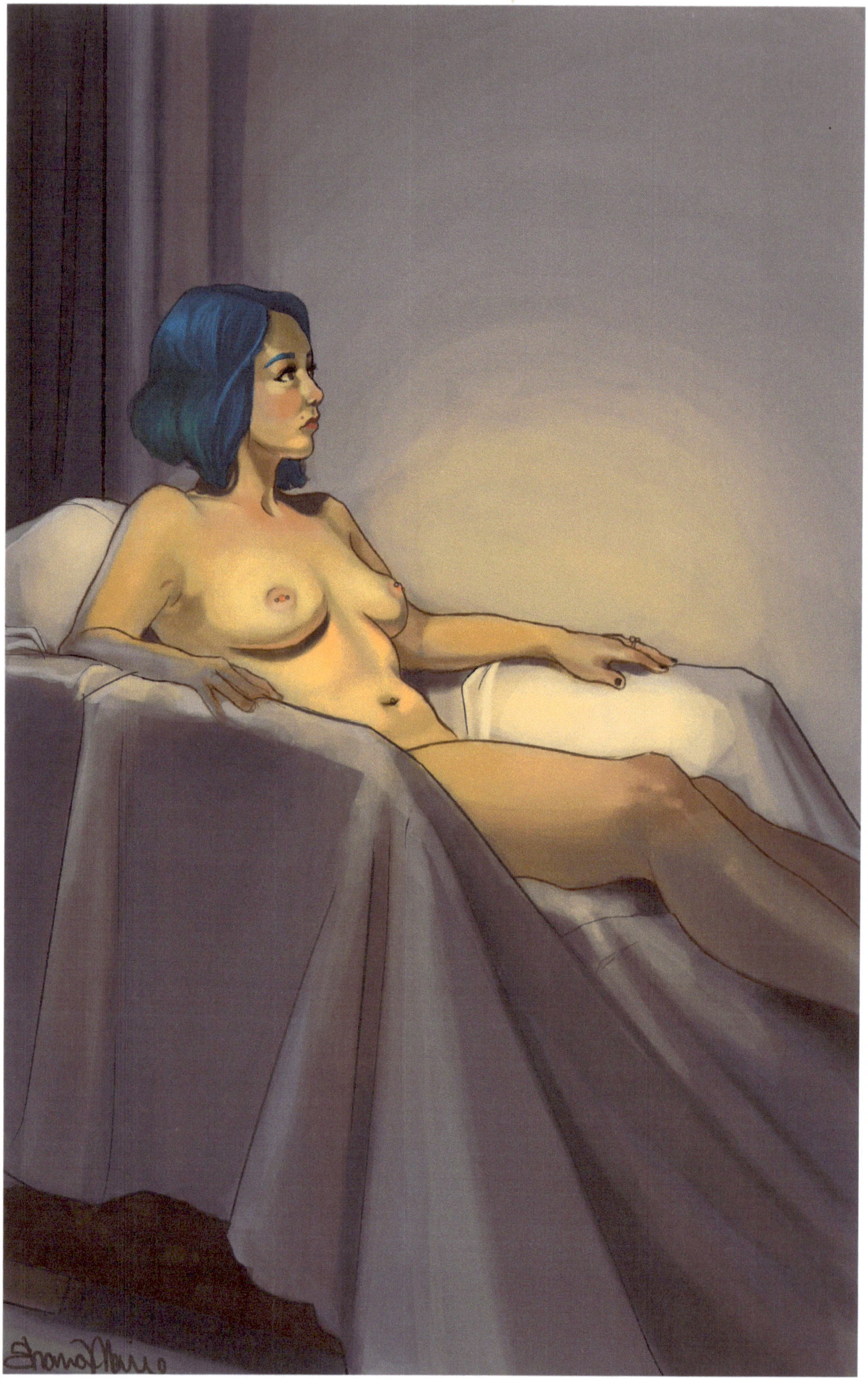

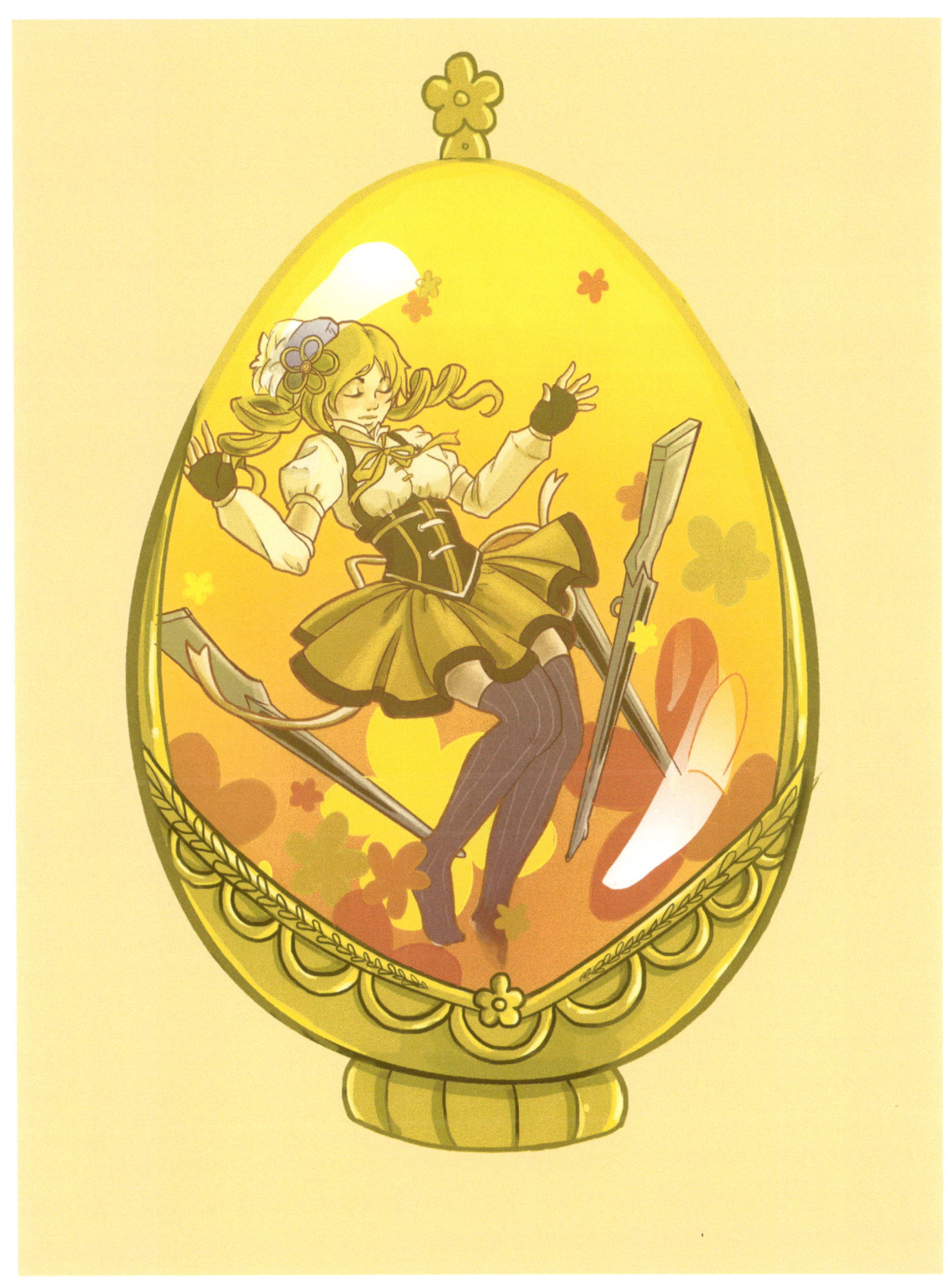

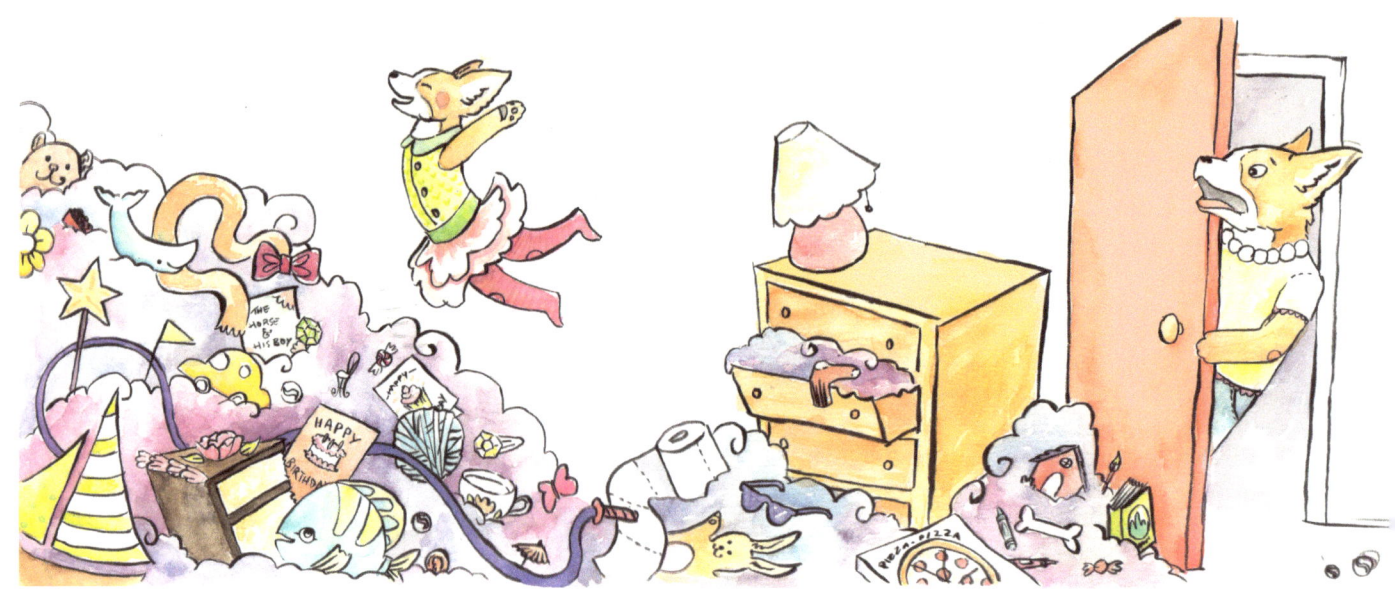

Anna Johnson | anna@annacj.com | annacj.com

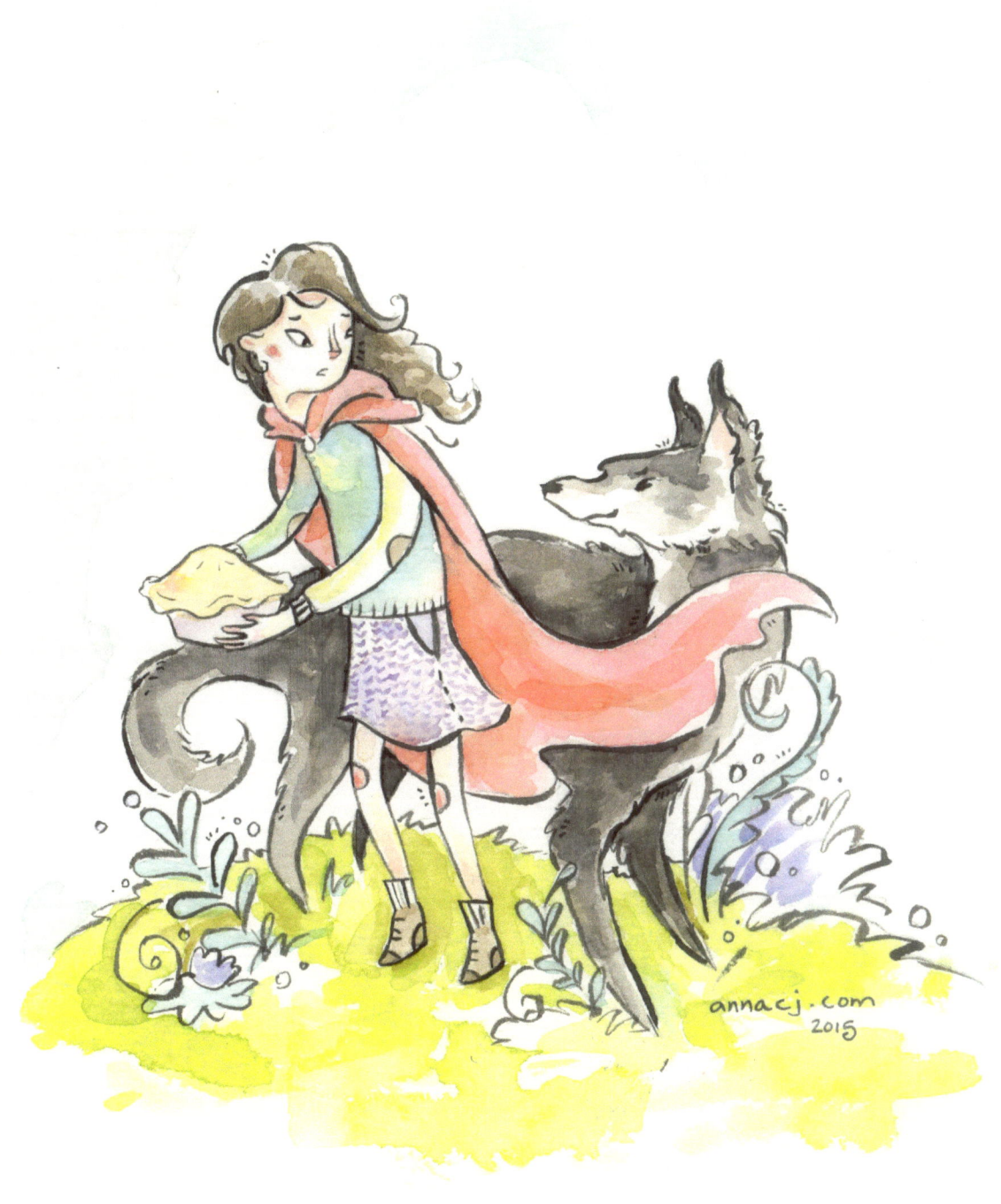

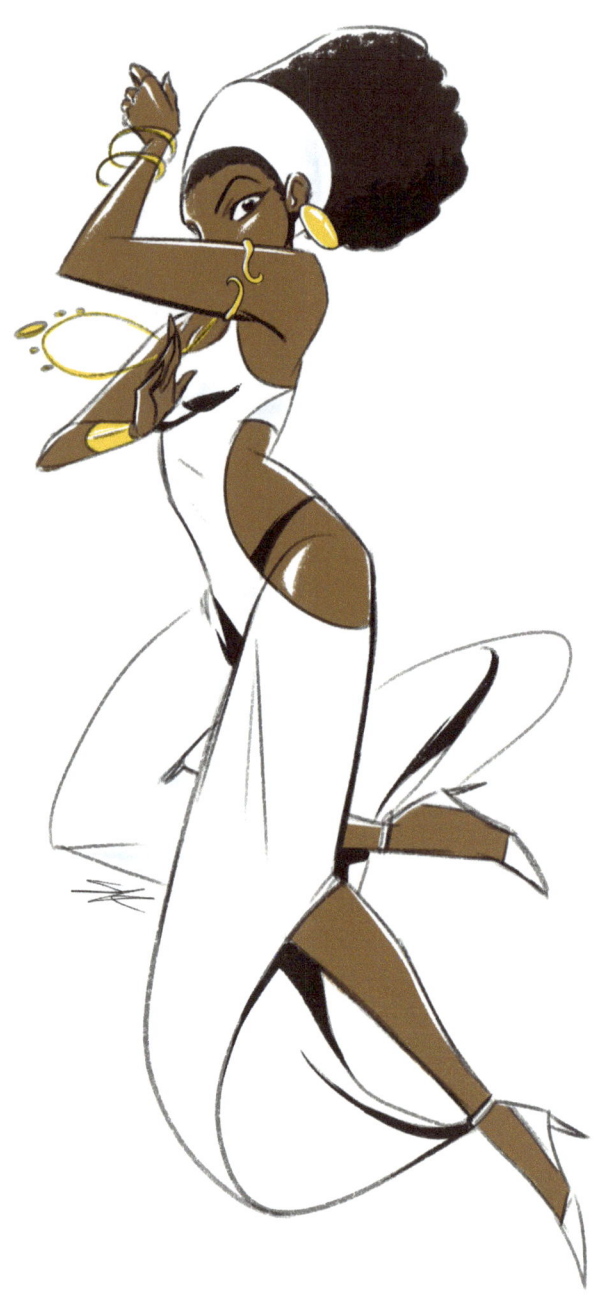

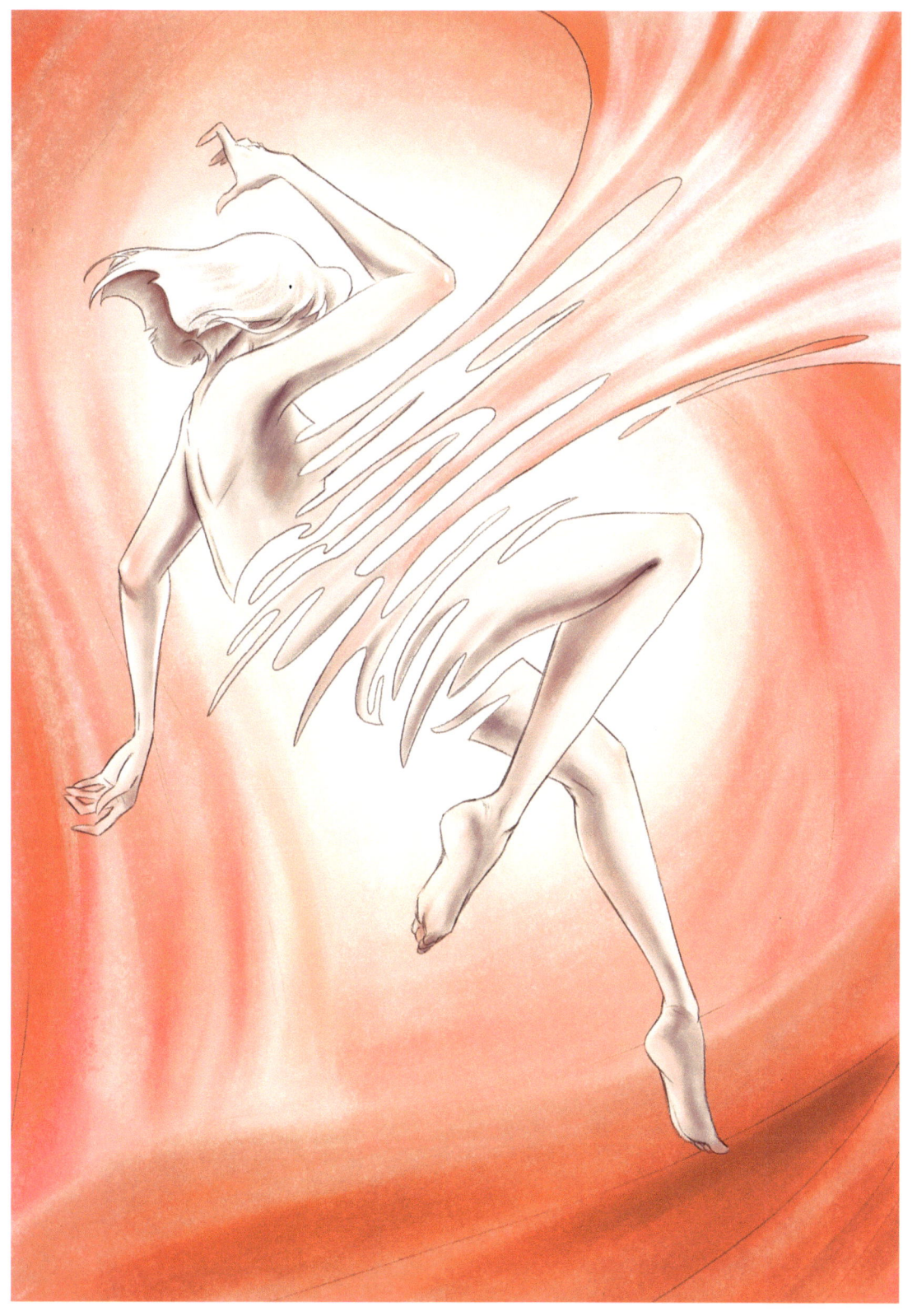

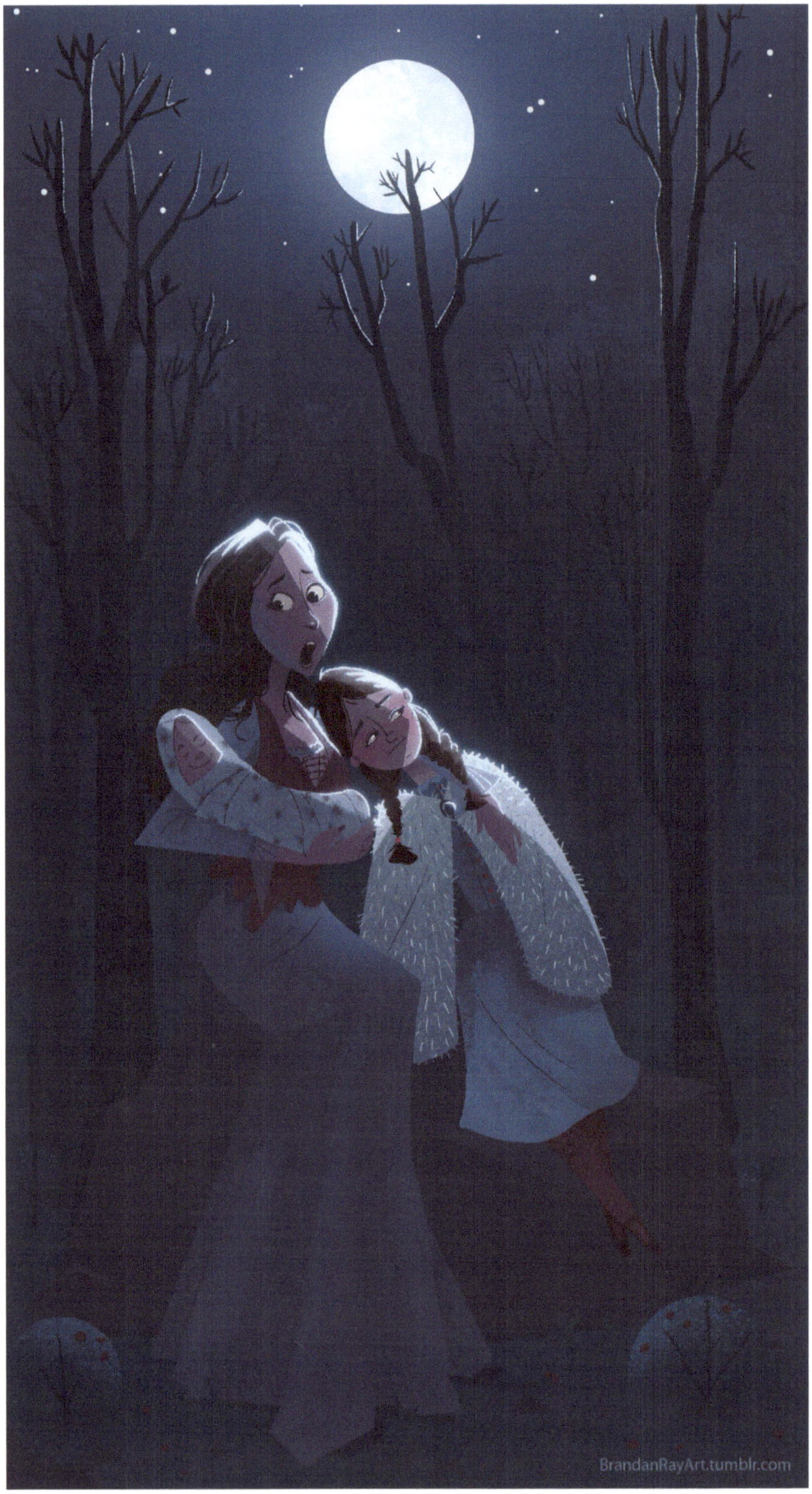

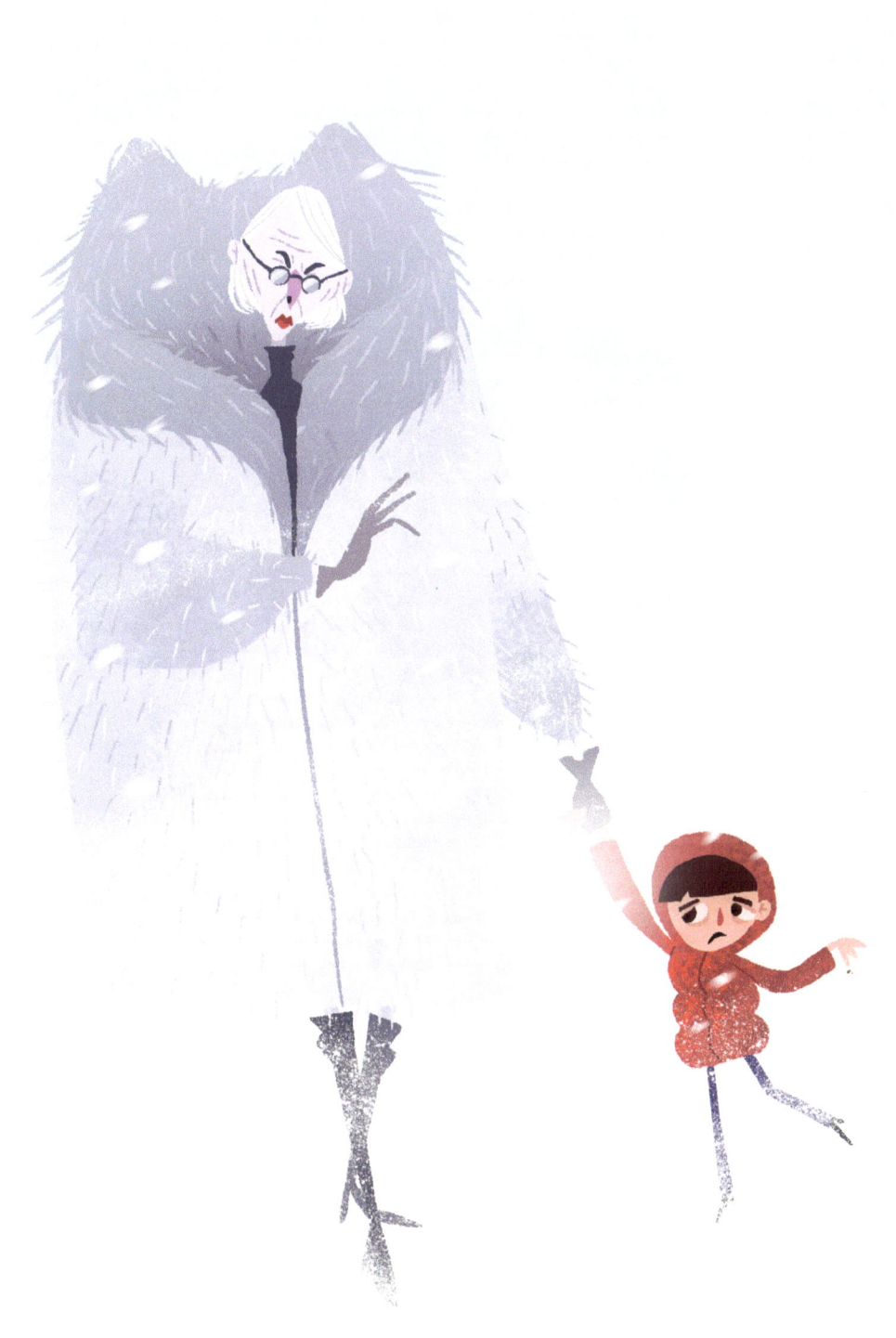

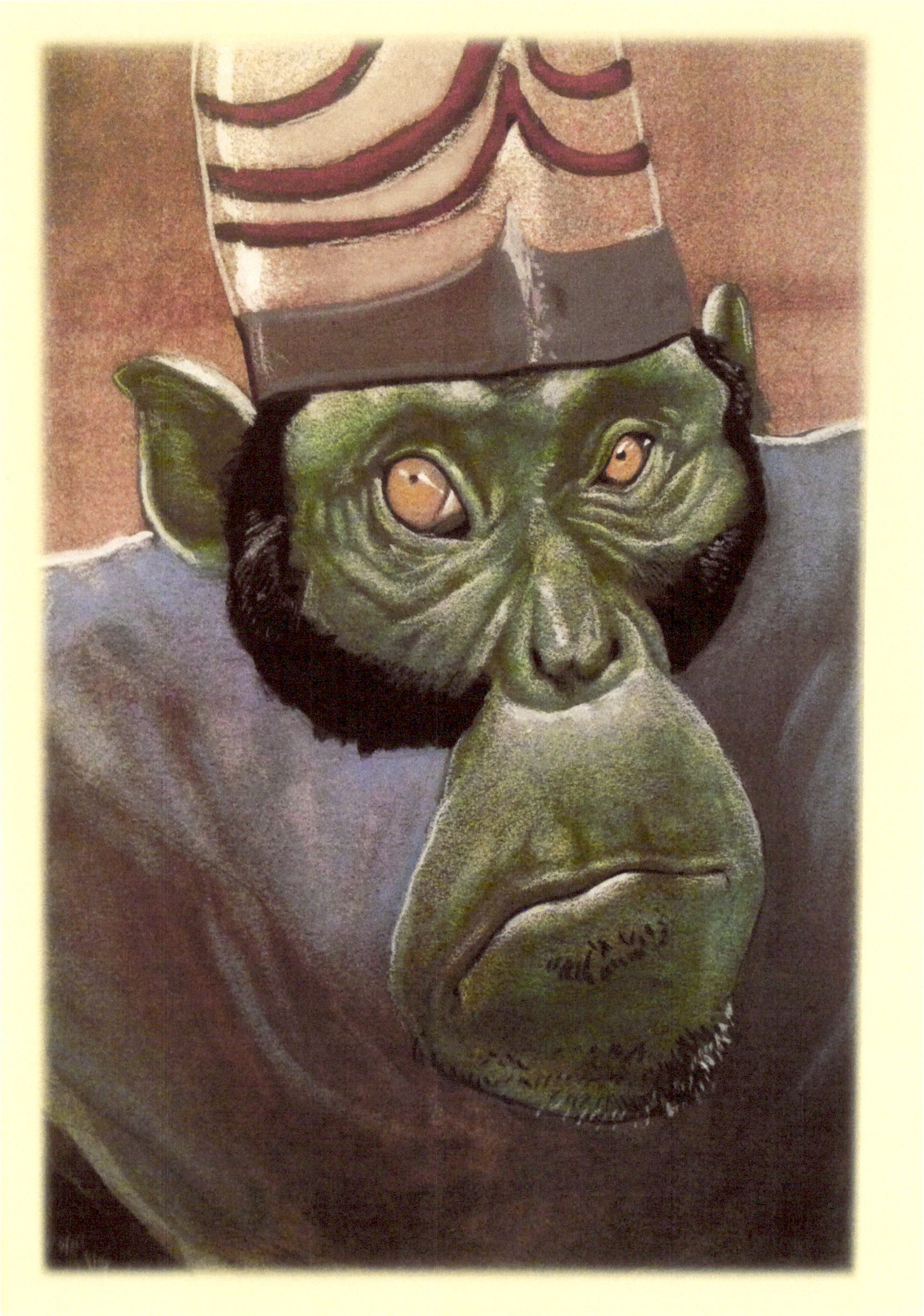

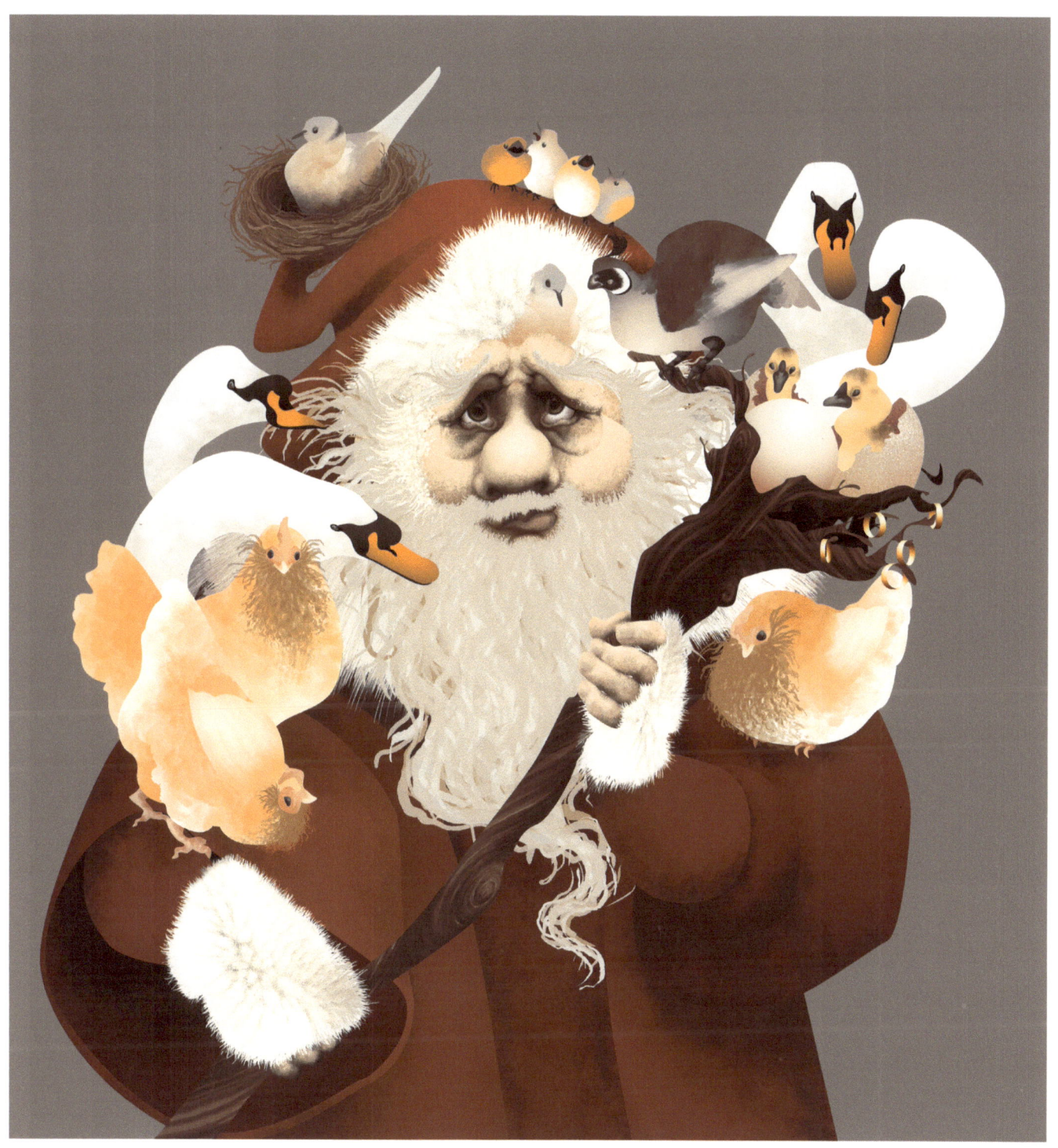

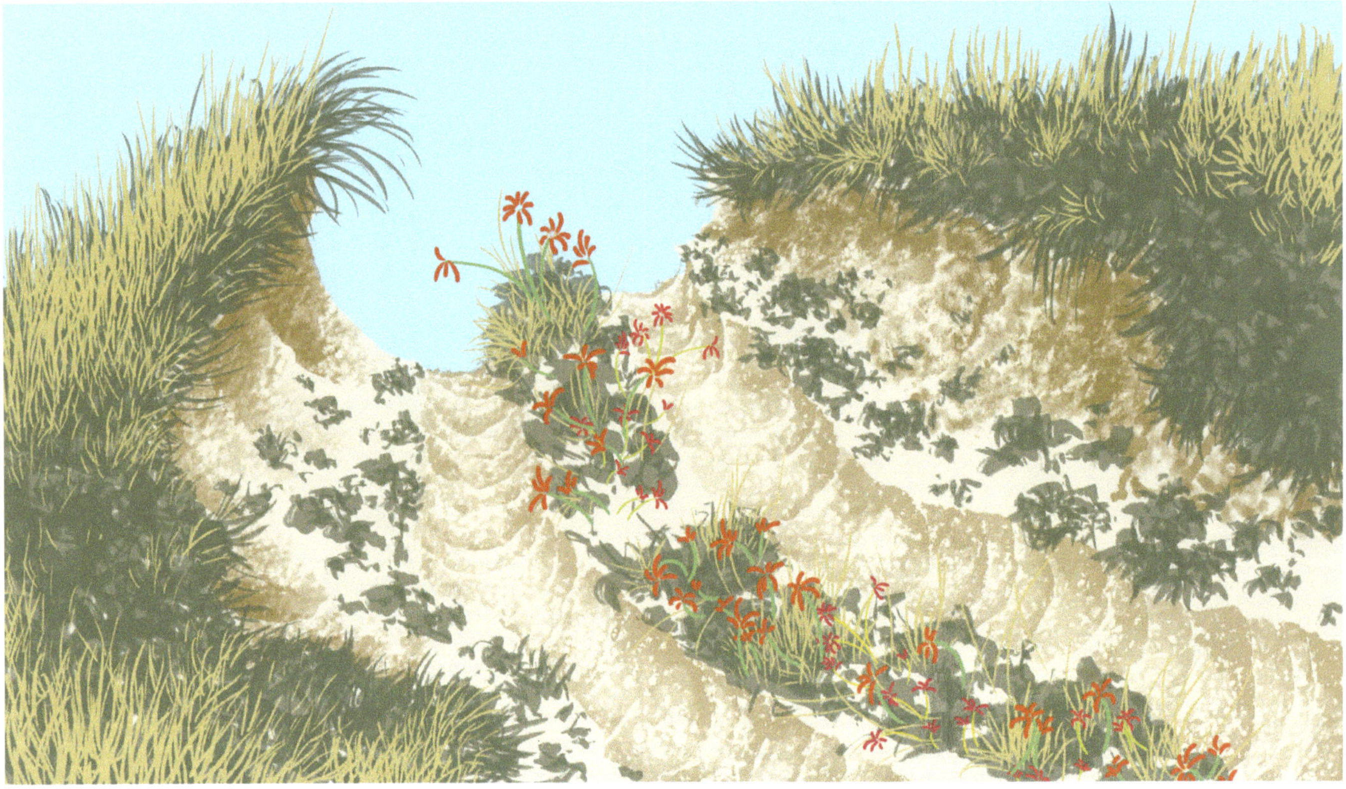

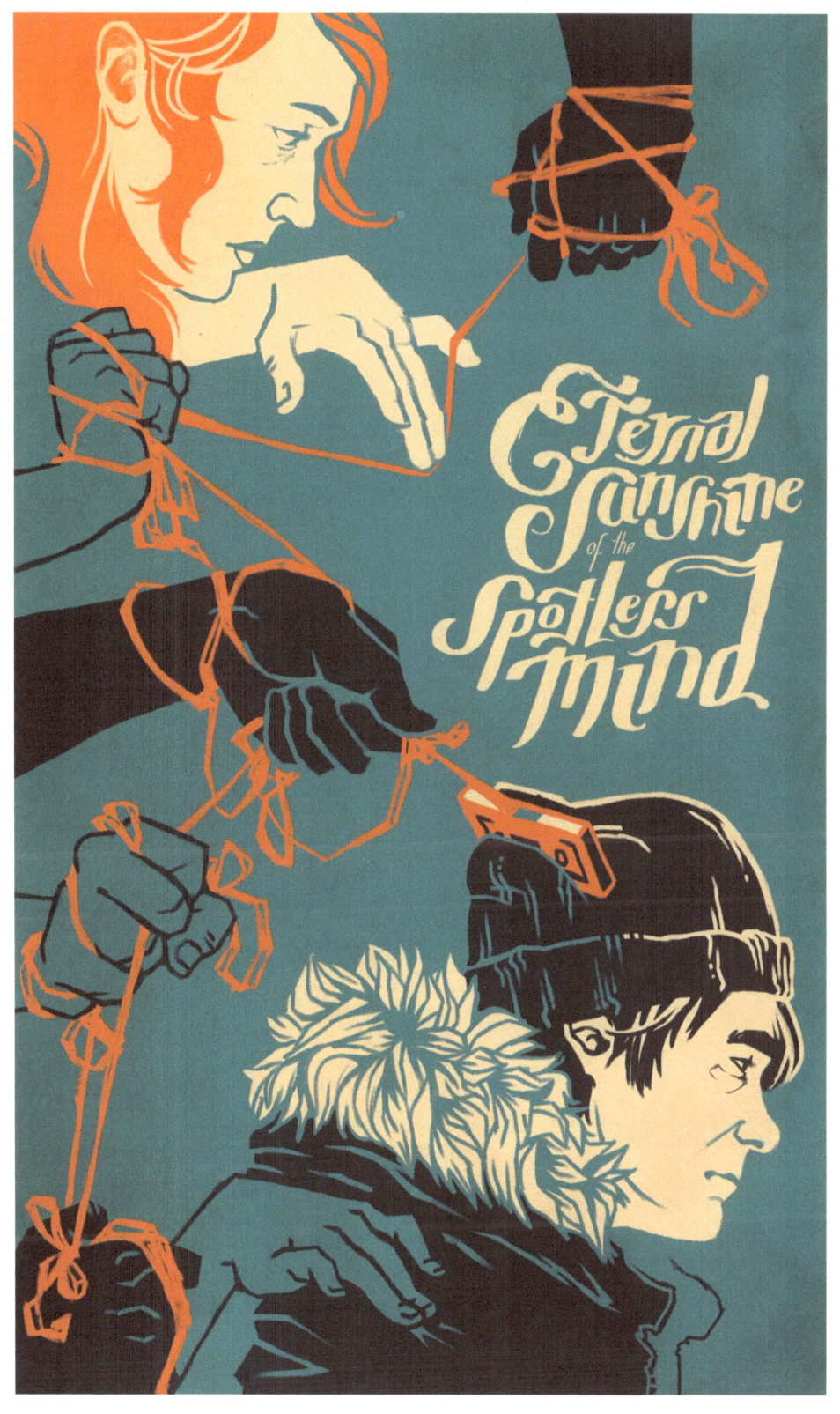

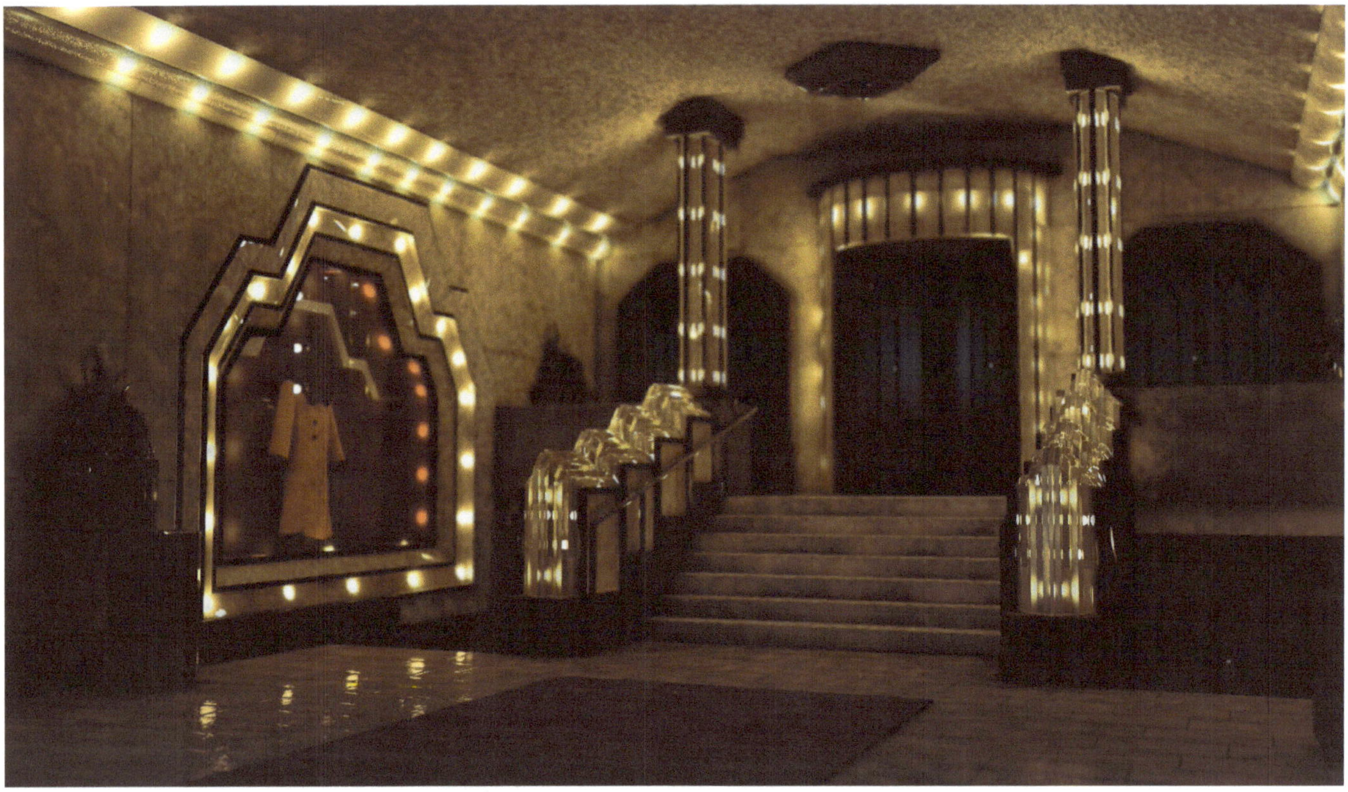

![Interior rendering of a lobby with lighted columns, a staircase, and an illuminated display window containing a coat]

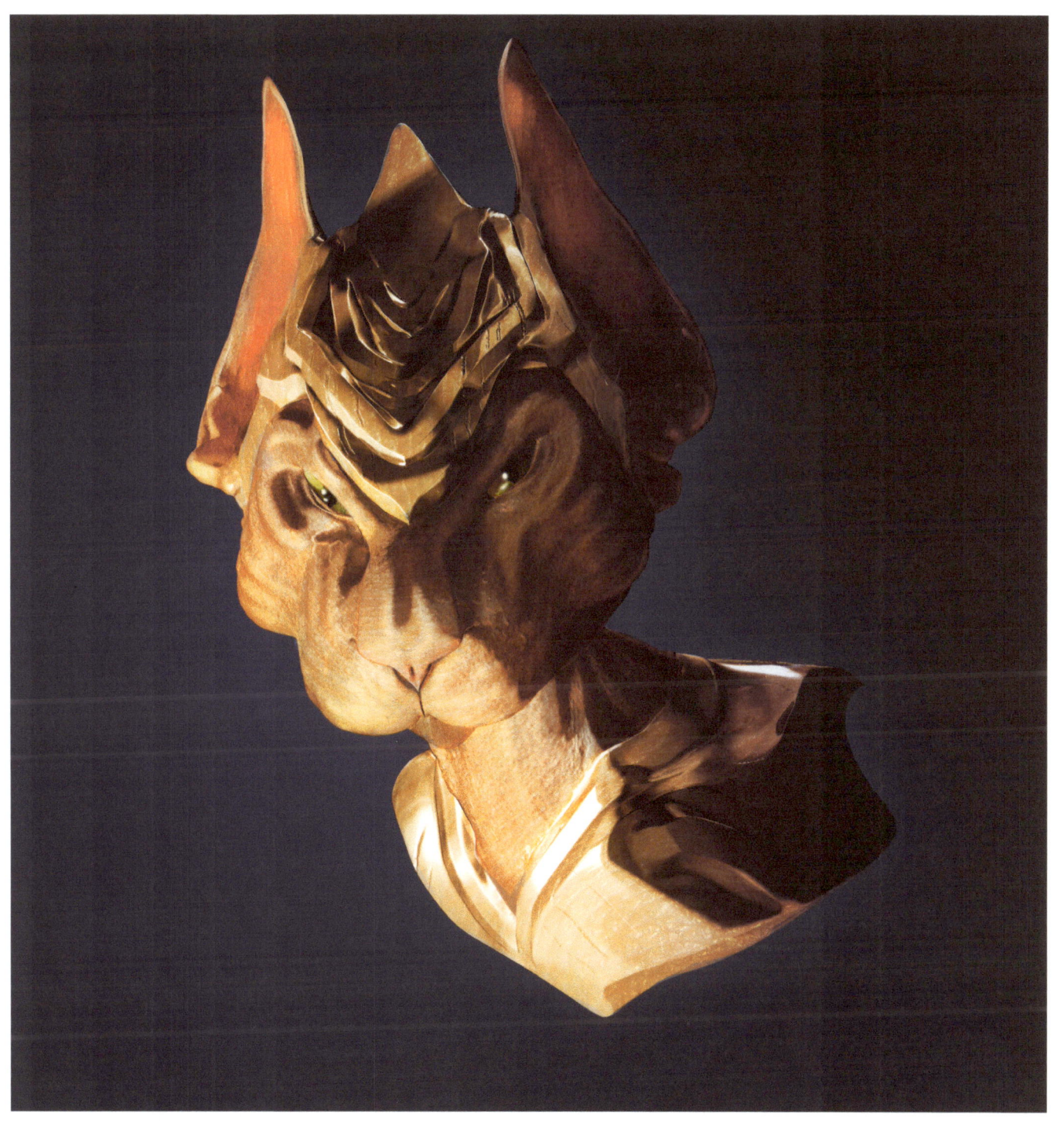

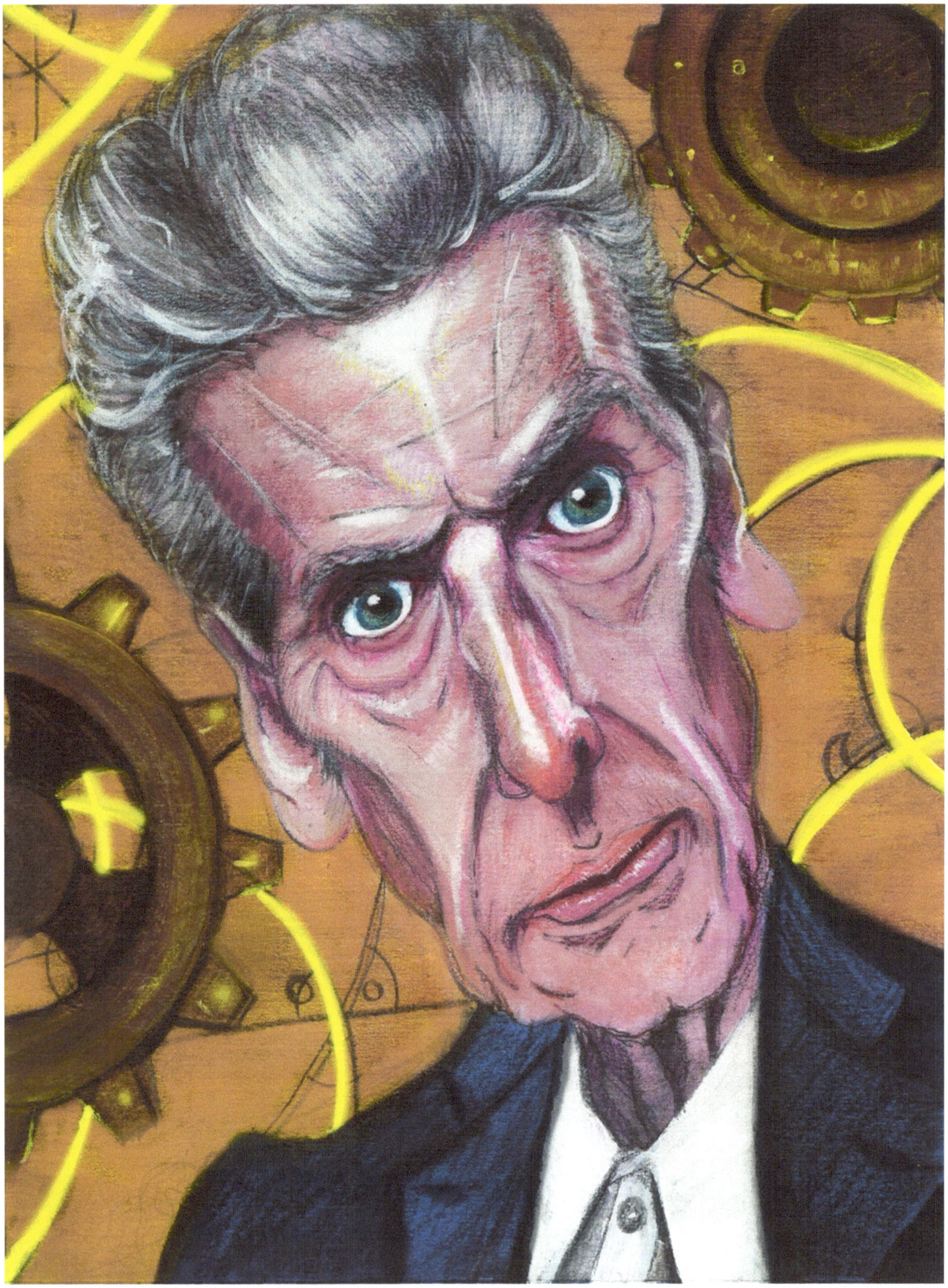

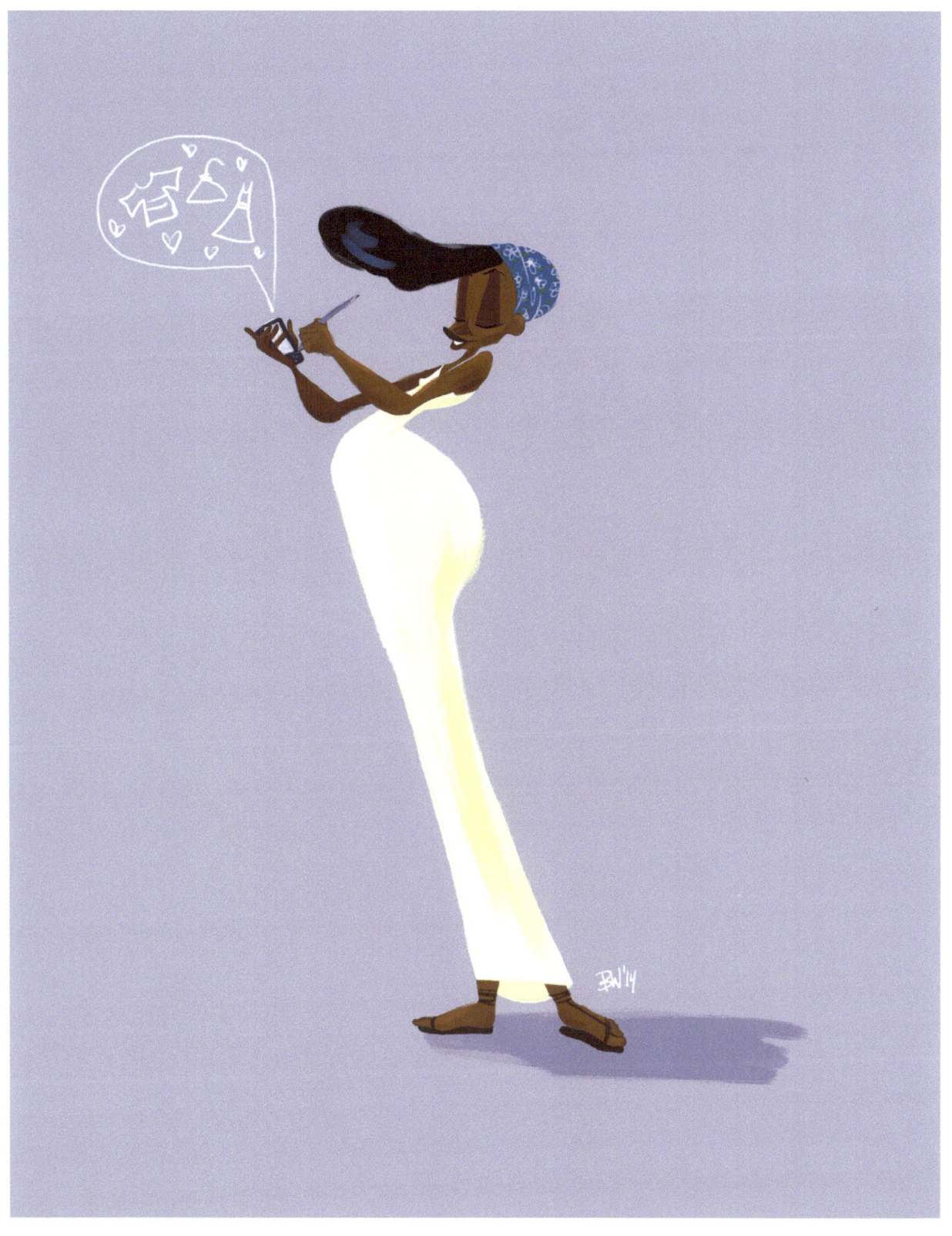

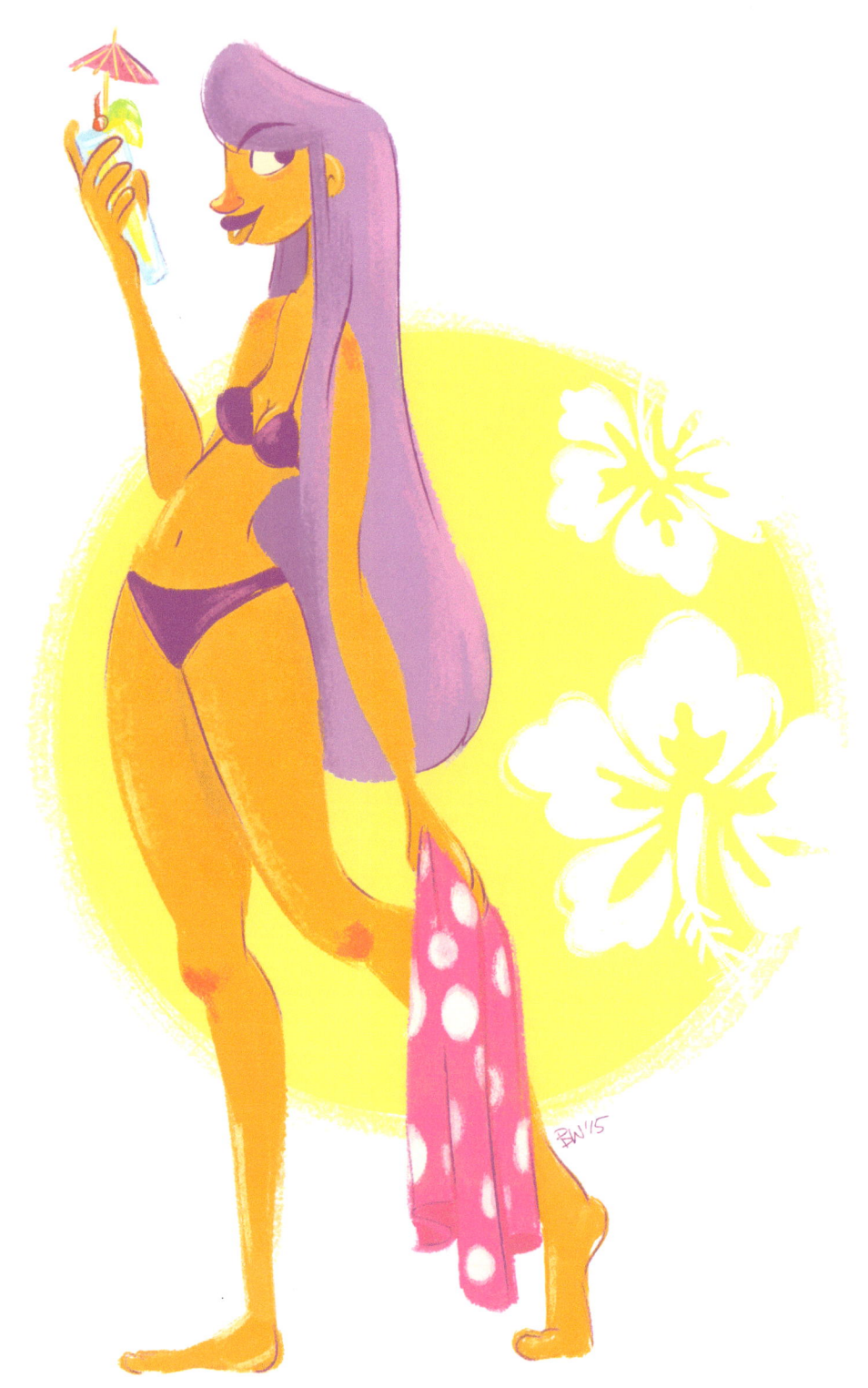

ACKNOWLEDGMENTS

This book was made possible by the
Illustration Student Collective Leaders of 2015.

Emmett Shearer – President
Ashley Tatman – Producer
Kevin Deasey – Art Director
Lauren Engle – Communications
Tyler Dunbar – Treasurer
Cat Tervo – President-in-Training
Shakir Smith – Producer-in-Training
Alec Valerius – Art Director-in-Training
Alexis Rampa – Communications and Treasurer-in-Training

We'd like to thank the Illustration Department of
Columbus College of Art & Design for their support.

We'd also like to thank our judges—Dave Groff, Jake
Mensinger, Adam Osgood, and Rebecca Zomchek—
all of whom are working as professional illustrators.
Their contribution in selecting these works has been
greatly appreciated.

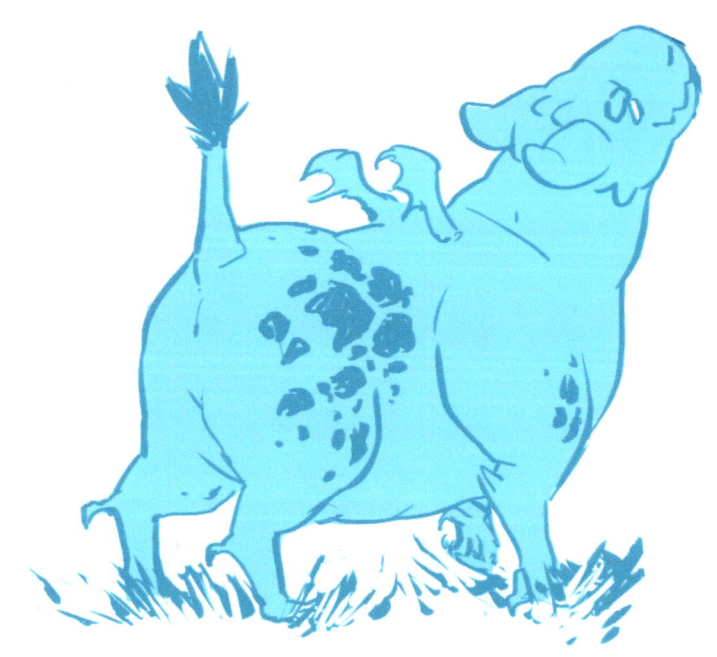

ABOUT THE COLLECTIVE

This group is dedicated to making students better illustrators by building professional practices, learning how to network, and improving their craft. Every week, ISC has guest speakers, workshops, tutorials, or homework/sketch parties. The group also coordinates gallery shows and runs social media outlets to provide members with additional ways to become involved.

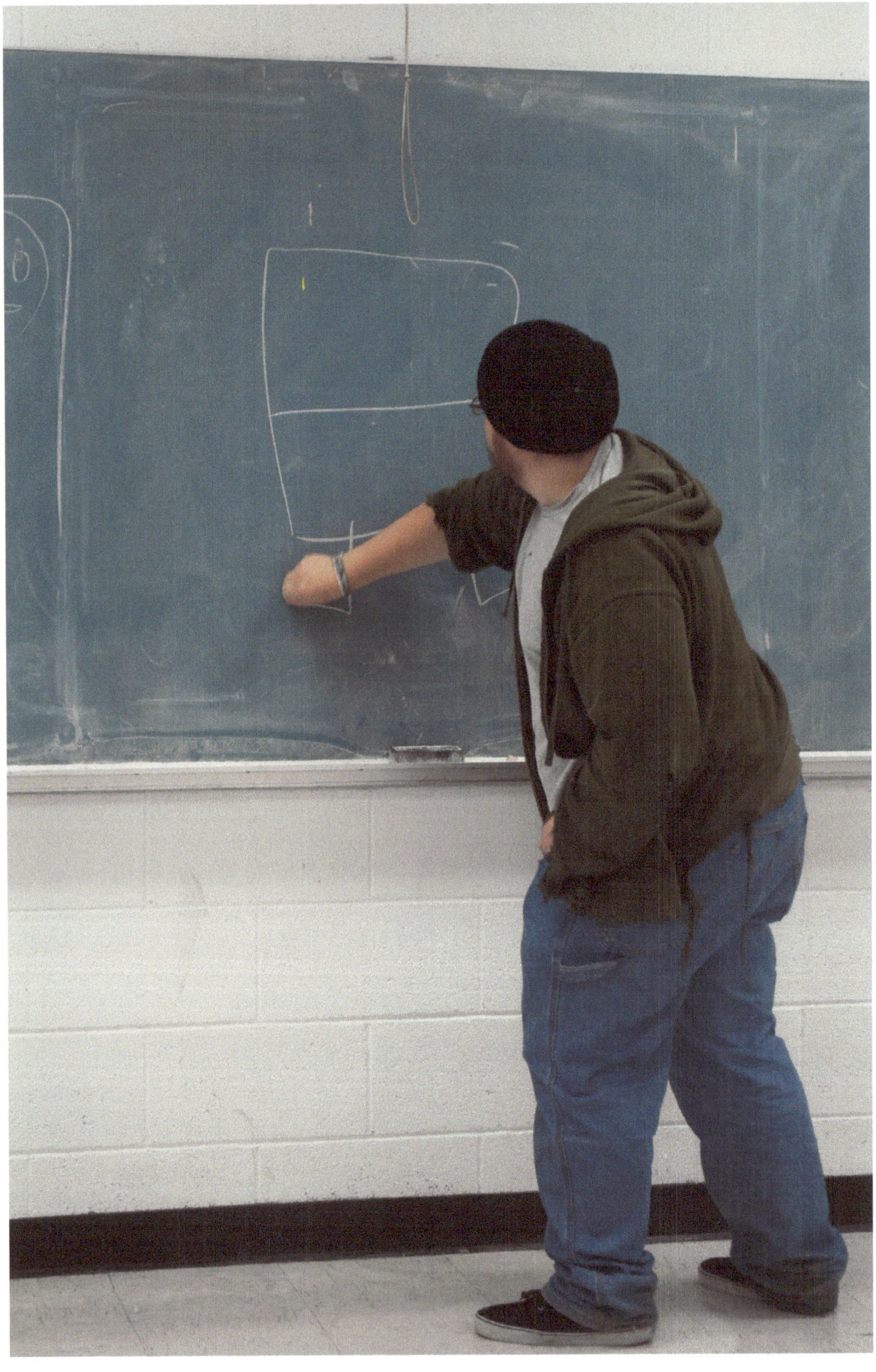

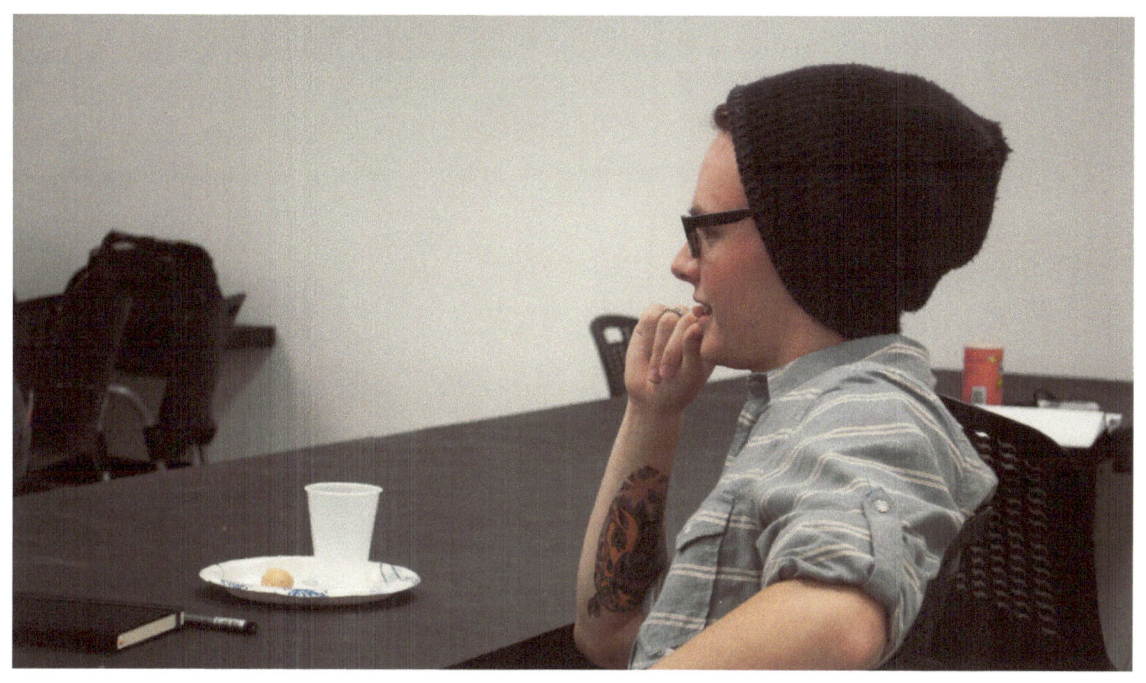

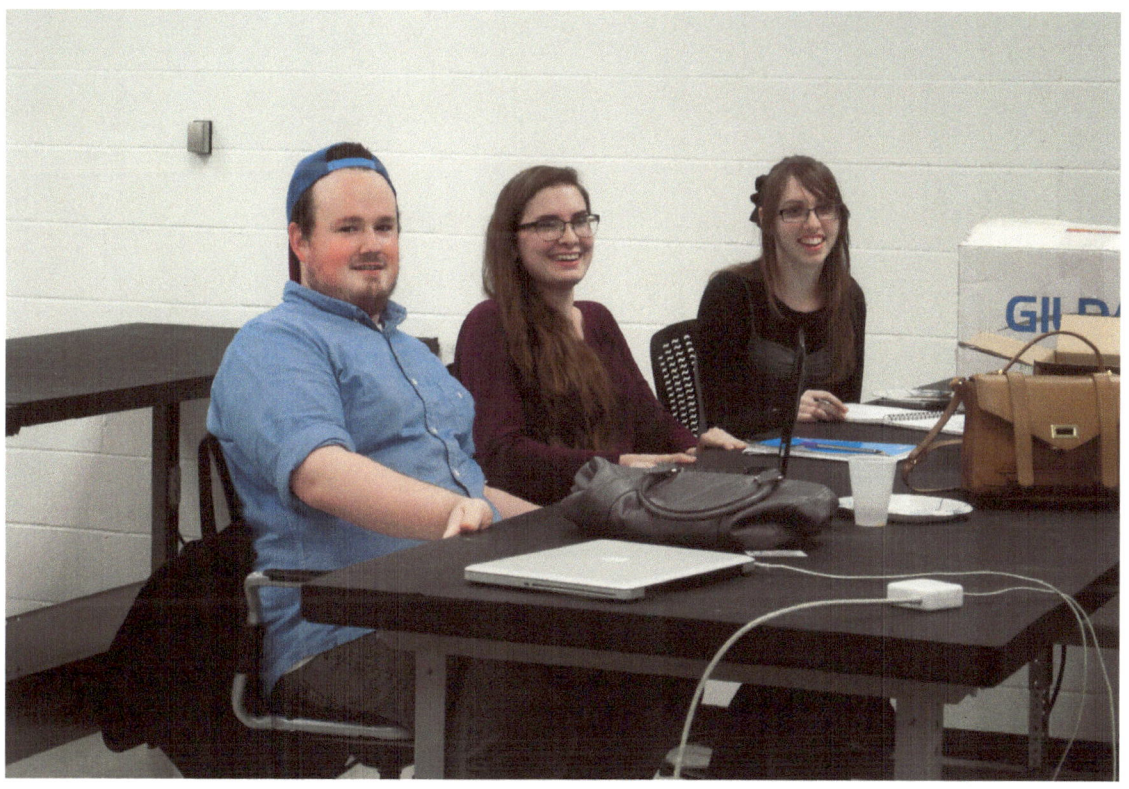

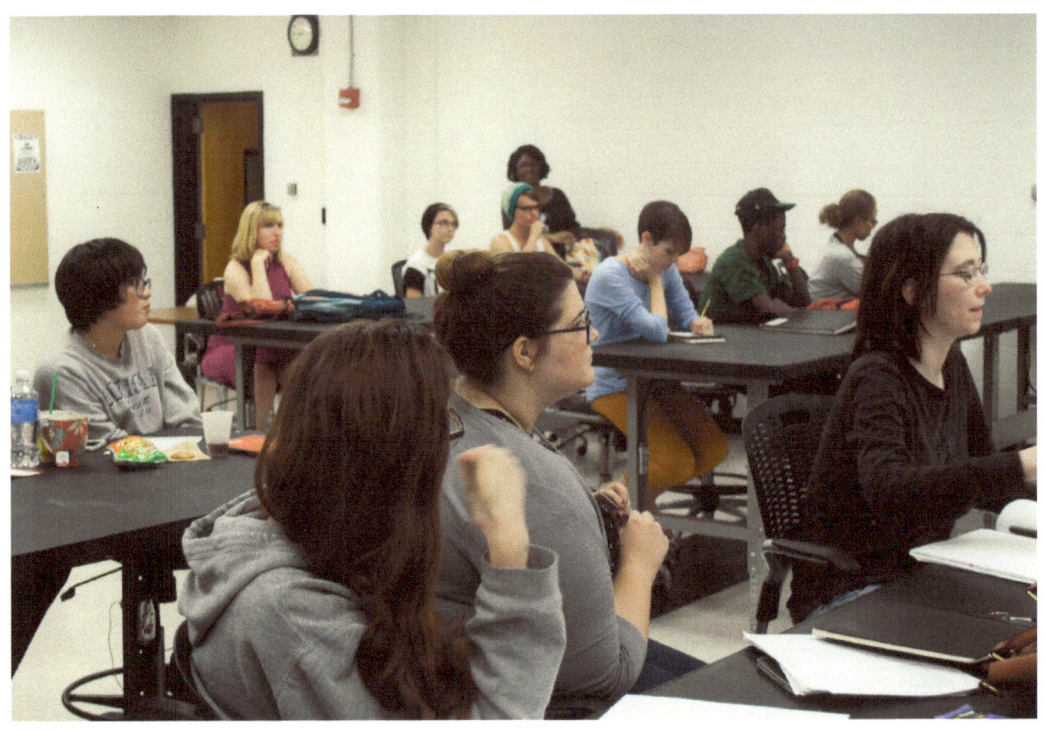

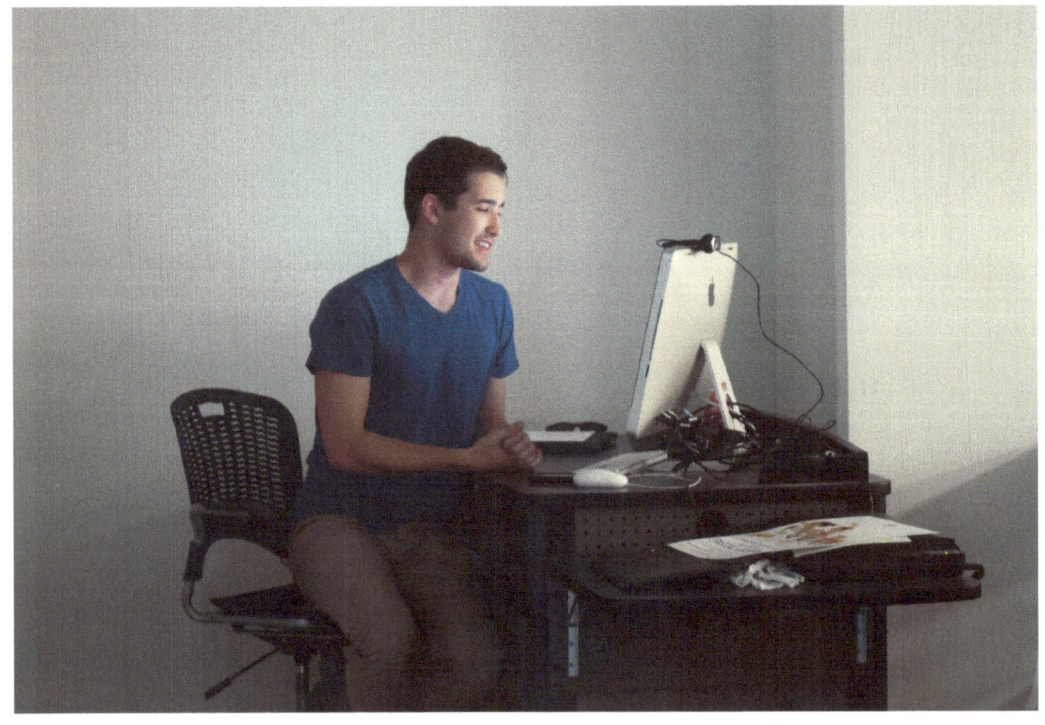

Skype Call with Pascal Campion

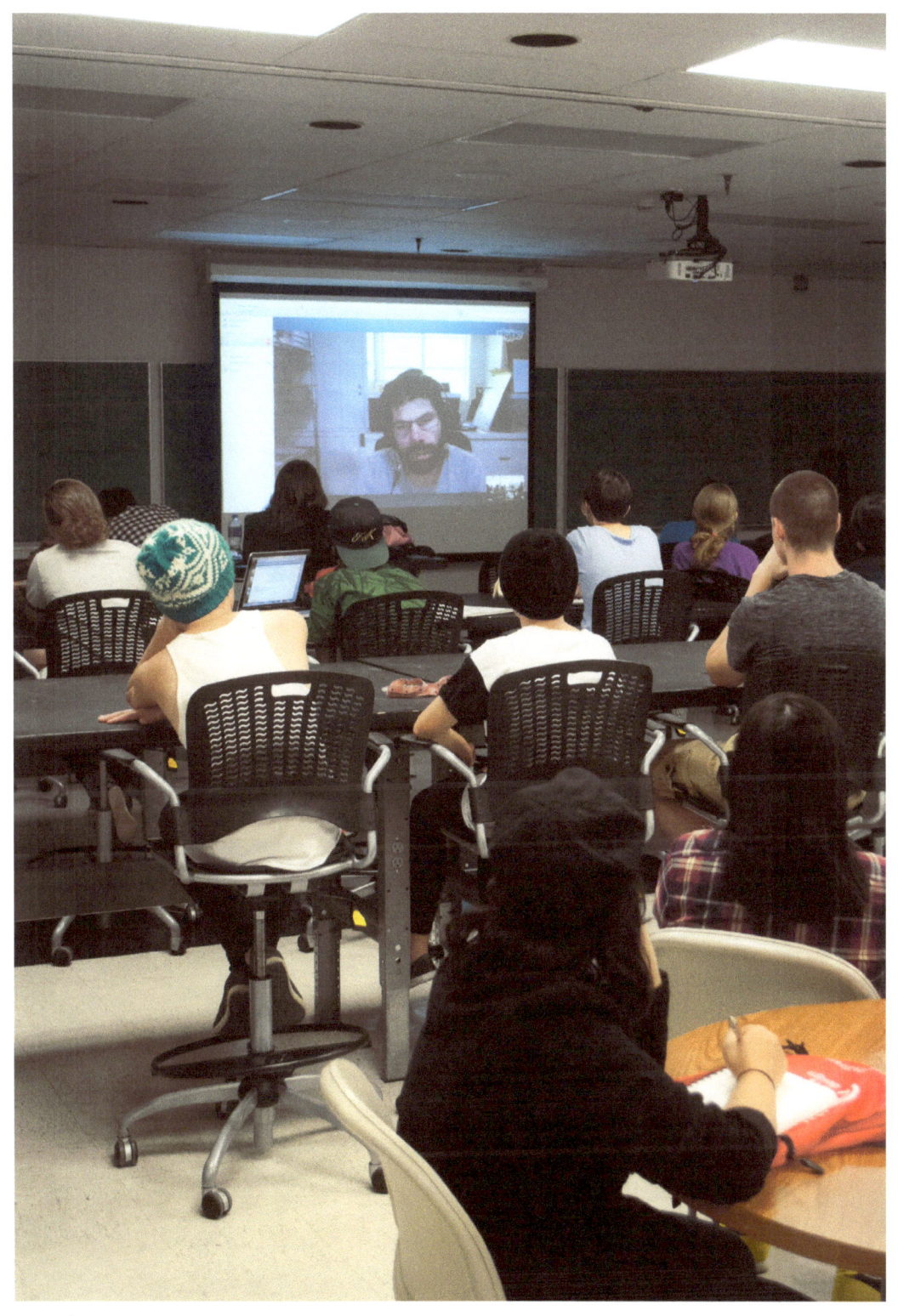

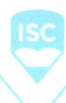

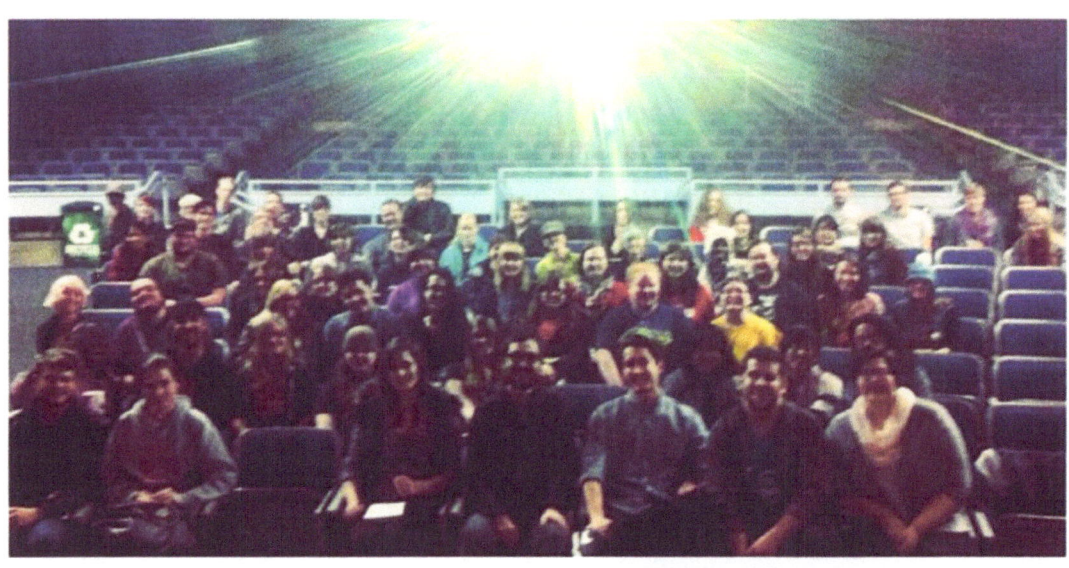

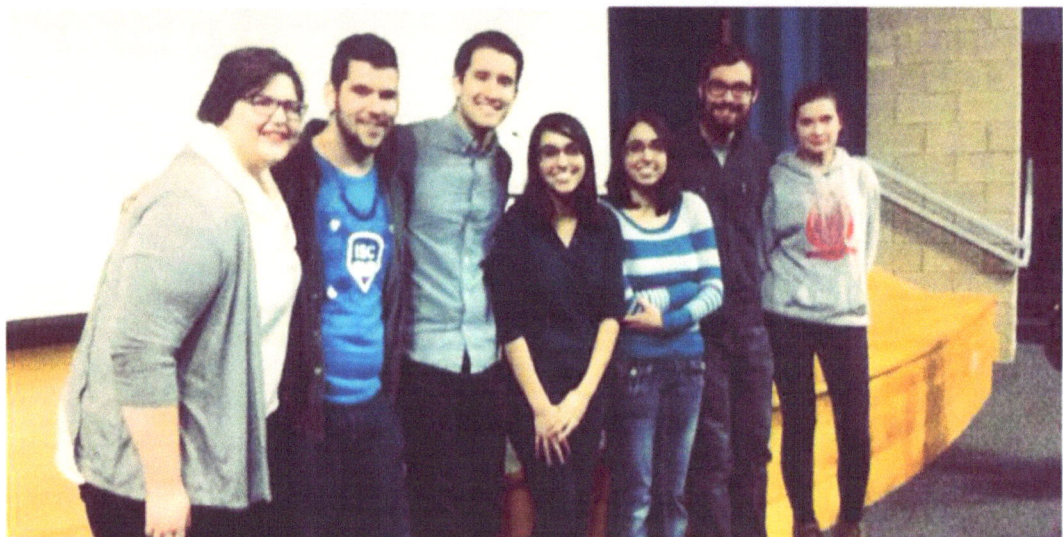

Visiting Artists Elena and Olivia Ceballos

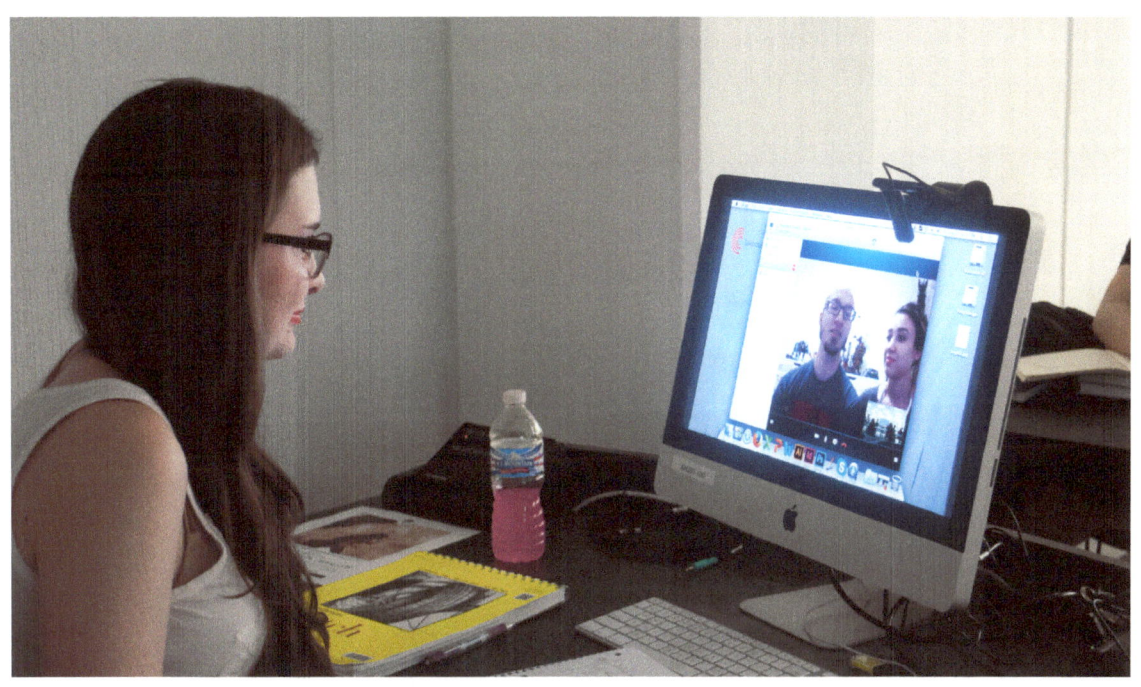

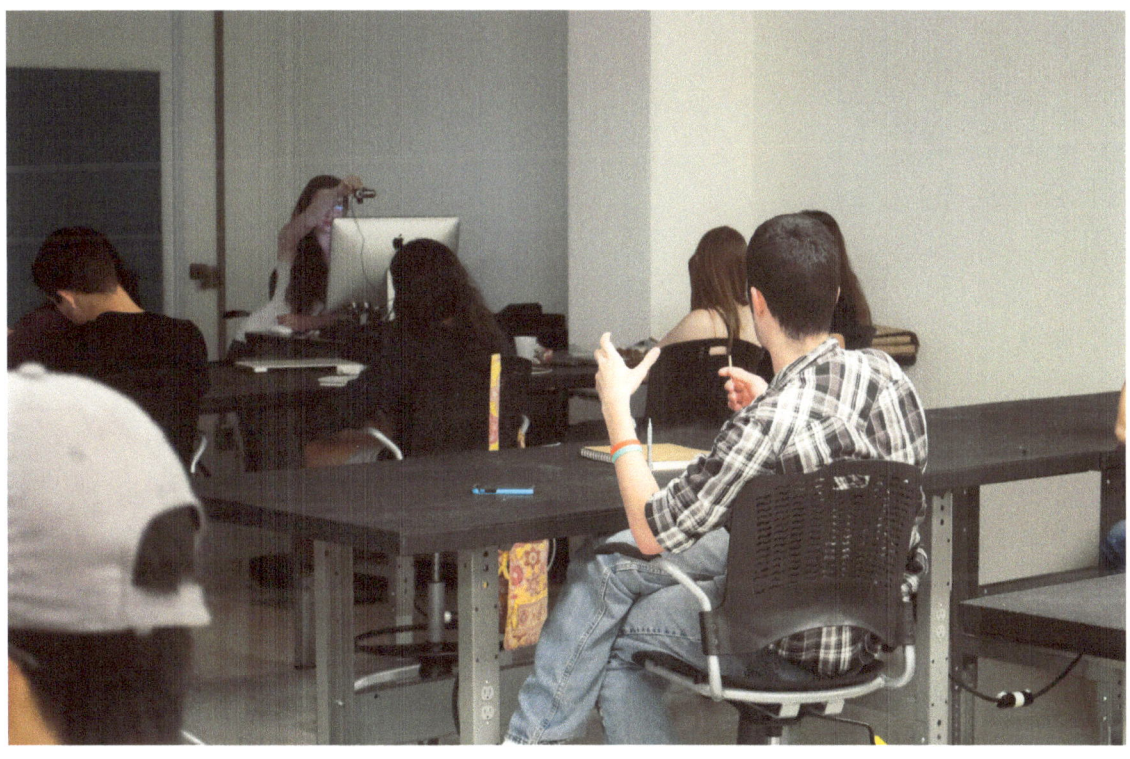

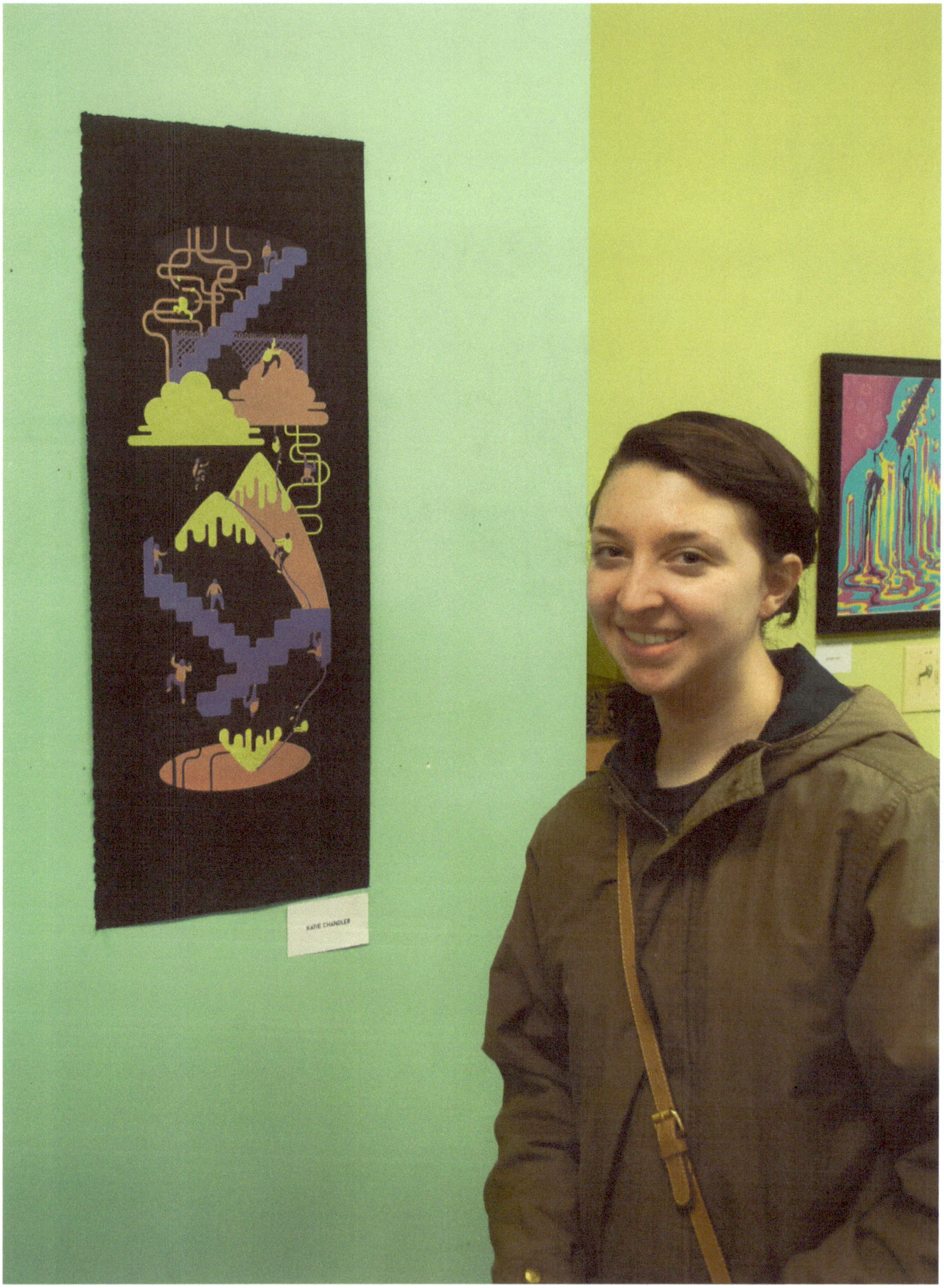

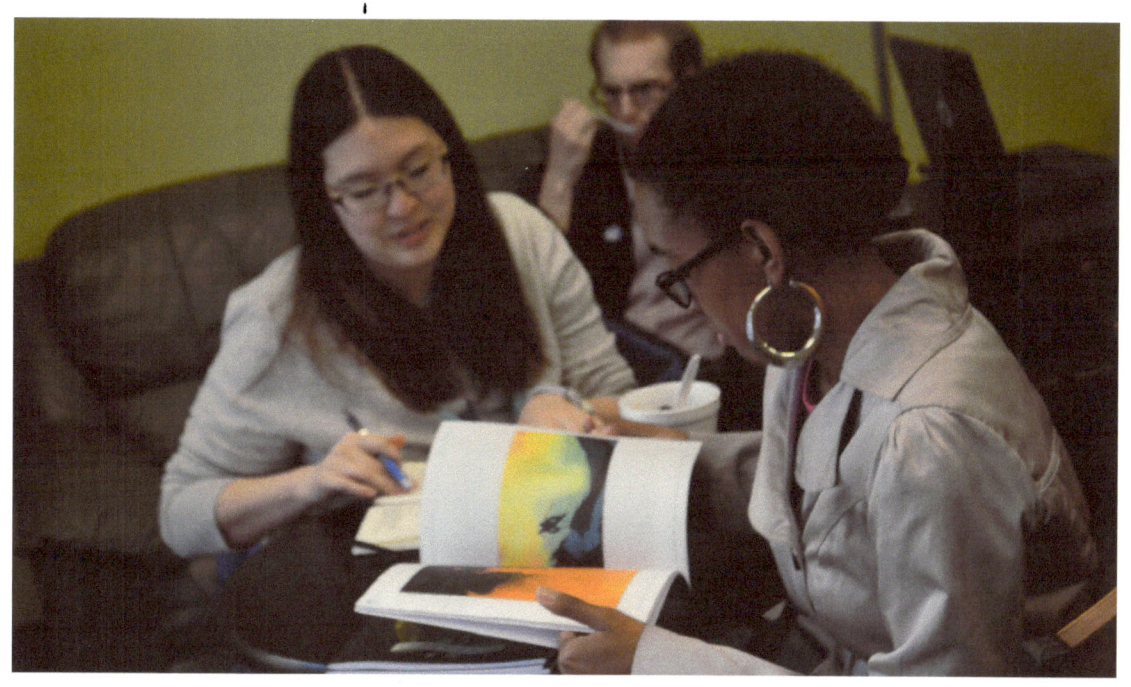

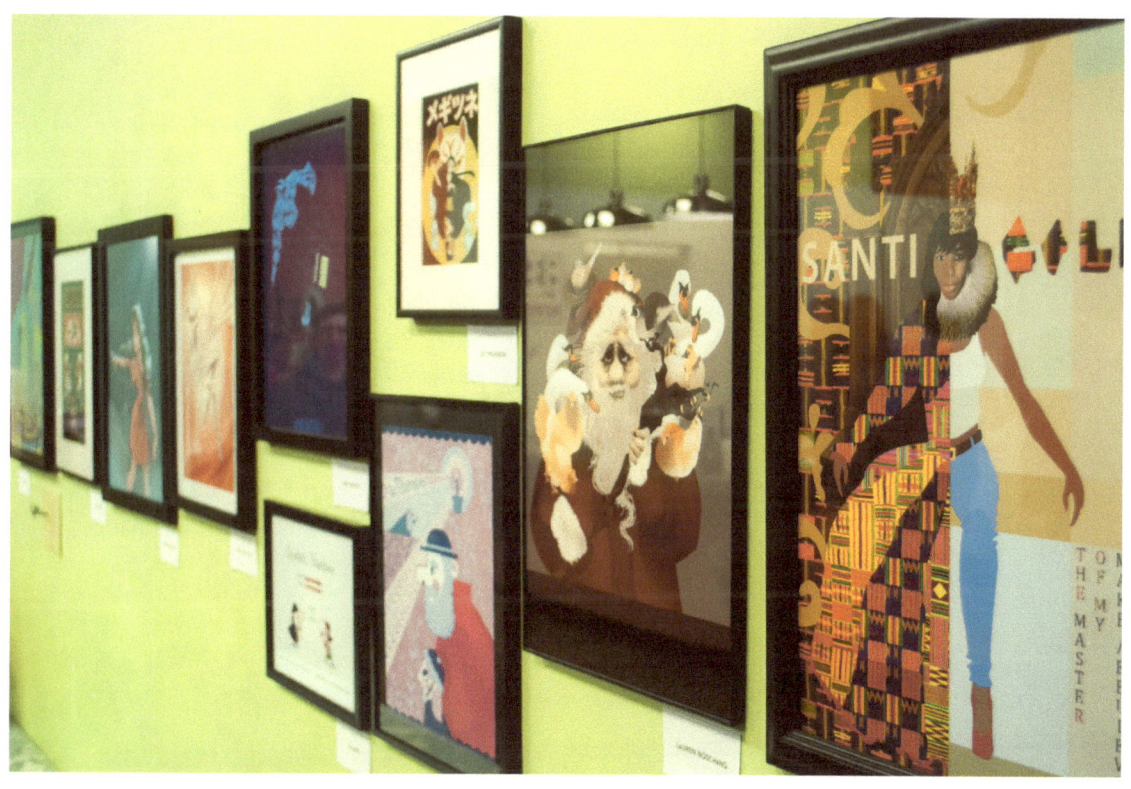

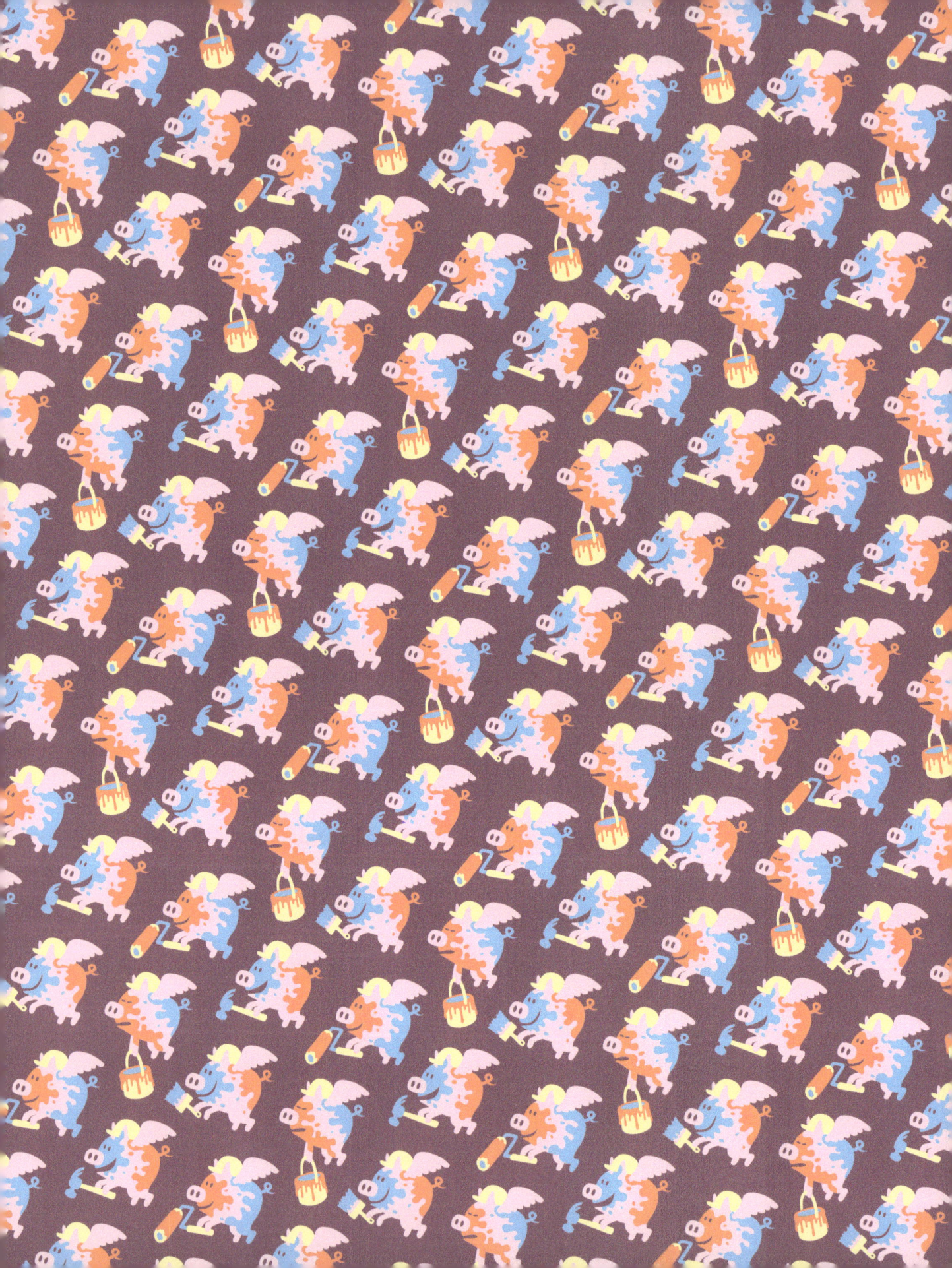

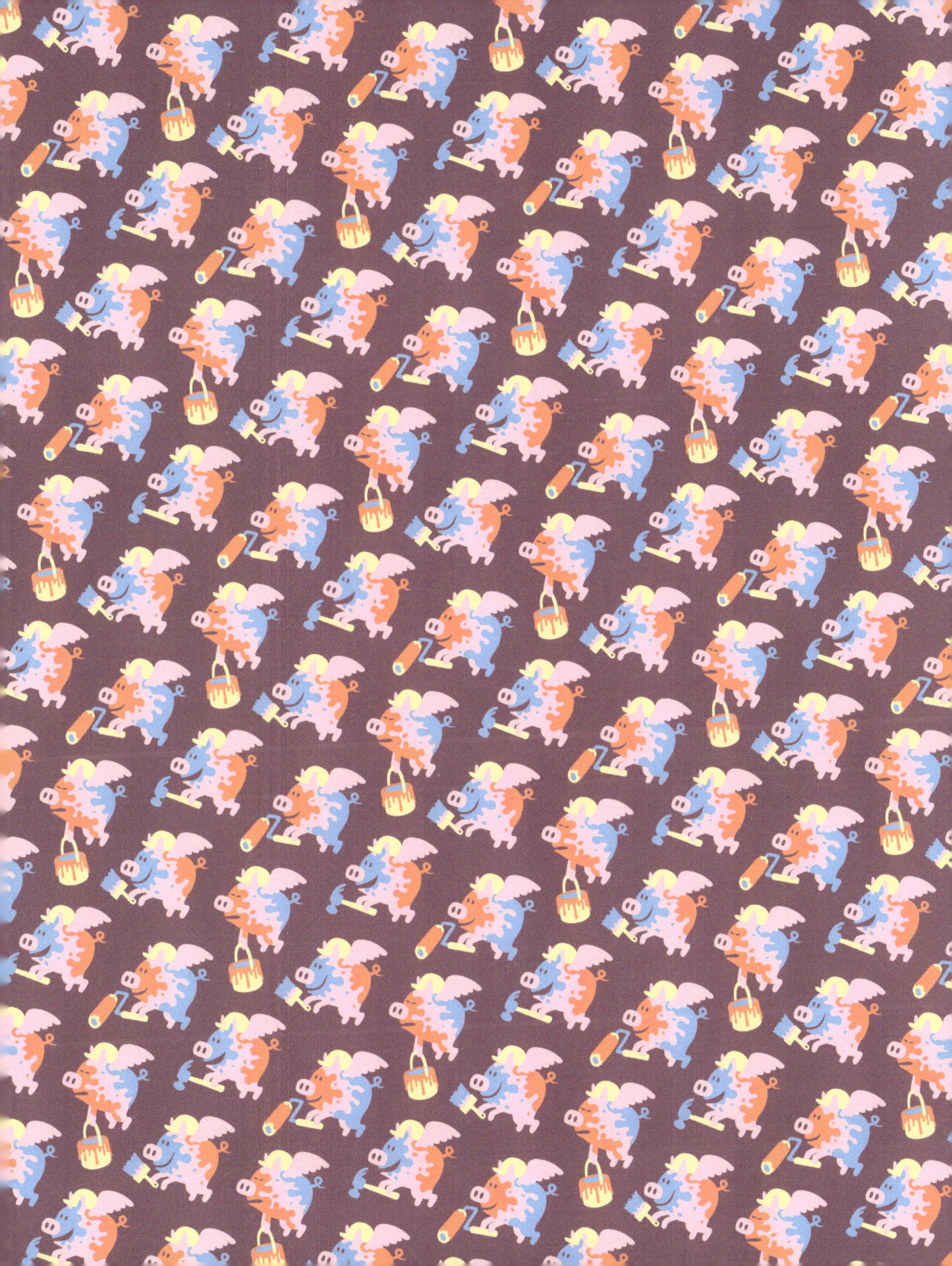

www.ingramcontent.com/pod-product-compliance
Lightning Source LLC
Chambersburg PA
CBHW050903180526
45159CB00007B/2770